Blackfeet Tales & Teachings
by John Tatsey

Introductions, translations and annotations by Mary Eggermont-Molenaar

Blackfeet Tales & Teachings in the Uhlenbecks' papers in the Congressional Record and in The Black Moccasin by John Tatsey

Introductions, translations and annotations
by Mary Eggermont-Molenaar

Copyright © 2019 by Mary Eggermont-Molenaar
Memo Books, Calgary AB.
ISBN: Soft Cover, 978-0-9812819-5-7

Layout: Colin McDonald

All rights reserved. No part of this book may be reproduced or transmitted in any form or by any means, electronic or mechanical, including photocopying, recording or by any information storage and retrieval system, without permission in writing from the publisher.

Also by
Mary Eggermont-Molenaar

Montana 1911: a Professor and his Wife among the Blackfeet
U of C / U of Nebraska Press, 2005

Missionaries among Miners, Migrants and Blackfoot
Calgary: U of C Press, 2007

Gustave Aimard: Feiten, Fictie, Frictie
Calgary: Special Snowflake, 2009

Hannah, Anna, Michael & Mary
Calgary: Memo Books, 2013

In en om de MMS te Huize Bijdorp, Voorschoten
Leiden: Uitgeverij Ginkgo, 2014

The William Van Horne Art Collection: A Dutch Treat
Calgary: Memo Books, 2014

Bij de Blackfeet in Montana in 1911: Dagboek van Willy Uhlenbeck-Melchior
Leiden: Uitgeverij Ginkgo, 2015

Veldwerkers en vrouwen in en om Baskenland
Leiden: Uitgeverij Ginkgo, 2018

Blackfeet Tales & Teachings

in the Uhlenbecks' papers
in the Congressional Record
and in The Black Moccasin
by John Tatsey

Introductions, translations and annotations by Mary Eggermont-Molenaar

Contents

Introduction 1

Part I
John Tatsey's Blackfeet tales and teachings
in the Uhlenbecks' papers. 5

Part II
John Tatsey's columns in the 1957-58
and 1969 *Congressional Record* 33
Part II Endnotes 45

Part III
The Black Moccasin 49
The Black Moccasin Endnotes 133

Let's finish 138
List of illustrations 143
Bibliography 145

Introduction

By the end of 1910, after having spent three months in a hospital in Conrad, Montana, 17-year old John Tatsey came home to his parents' tipi at the Blackfeet Reservation in Montana. Months earlier a wild horse had hit and hurt him, but now but he could walk again. At the entrance of the tipi of his parents, Joe and Annie Tatsey, he saw a white man and heard him ask his father whether "that boy was another one of yours."

One year later, in 1911, that same white man, Dr. C. C. Uhlenbeck from the Netherlands was back at the Blackfeet Reservation. In 1910 he had been there with his student Jan de Josselin de Jong; this time he brought along his wife Willy Uhlenbeck-Melchior. John Tatsey would become one of Uhlenbeck's very much appreciated consultants on his efforts to learn the Blackfoot language.

During the three months of their stay at the Blackfeet Reservation Mrs. Uhlenbeck kept a diary. Her diary entrees enable us to see how John Tatsey's tales and teachings for her husband came about. When the Ulenbecks left the reservation in September 1911, it was John who brought them to the Browning railway station by horse and buggy. When they took leave of each other, John promised to write the couple. Whether that happened we don't know. But we do know that later in life John became a rancher, moved on to become a policeman and did write; he became a columnist for the *Glacier Reporter* and the *Hungry Wolf*.

John's columns drew the attention of Mike Mansfield, from 1952 representing the State of Montana in the Senate. Later on, in his capacity of Senate Majority Leader he addressed "Mr. President" twice, requesting to have few of Tatsey's columns reprinted in the *Congressional Record*.

Tatsey's columns in the *Congressional Record* might have drawn the attention of Paul Devore, journalist and once editor at the *Helena Independent* and the *Great Falls Tribune*. In 1971, two years after Tatsey's columns appeared in the *Congressional Record,* Devore compiled and edited a number of these columns, added Tatsey's tales and teachings and published this collage as *The Black*

Moccasin. This treasure illustrated with photographs by Wayne Curtis and drawings by Albert Racine is no longer in print.

In Part I of *Blackfeet Tales and Teachings* John Tatsey's stories in Uhlenbeck's 1912 and 1920 publications are reprinted, preceded by Mrs. Uhlenbeck's diary entrees and few of the photographs she took.

Tatsey's columns in the 1957 and 1969 *Congressional Record*, preceded by introductions, are reprinted and make up Part II of this book.

Part III presents the complete texts and illustrations of *The Black Moccasin*. Brian Kavanagh, owner of the *Cut Bank Pioneer Press,* under which the *Glacier Reporter* currently resorts, kindly granted permission for the columns in it and Carol Murray-Tatsey, John's granddaughter, for the tales and teachings part thereof.

Here I thank John's granddaughter Carol Murray-Tatsey for her graceful co-operation as well as Brian Kavanah for his consent to republish *The Black Moccasin* and John McGill of *Glacier Reports,* for a part of his 2012 newspaper article in which John Tatsey is mentioned.

Mary Eggermont-Molenaar,
Calgary, 2018

Part I

John Tatsey's Blackfeet tales and teachings in the Uhlenbecks' papers

C. C. Uhlenbeck: Why did, C. C. Uhlenbeck (1866-1951), professor in Old-Germanic Languages at University Leiden, the Netherlands, over one hundred years ago come to the Blackfeet Reservation?[1] Who was he? Where did he look for at the Blackfeet Reservation? Uhlenbeck was born in the Dutch city of Haarlem where he had a troublesome youth. His father, a failed businessman, had taken it upon himself to invent and construct an airplane something in which he did not succeed. As his parents lost several of their children at a very young age, Uhlenbeck grew up as an only child. Disappointment must have hovered over

Uhlenbeck and his wife Willy Uhlenbeck-Melchior around 1900.

---

1. Blackfeet is the name of the tribe in Montana. Blackfoot is the spelling of their language and also the umbrella name of the Canadian tribes, the Blood, Peigan and Siksika, and that with the Tsuu T'Ina and the Stoneys form the Blackfoot Confederation. The American tribe of the Blackfoot Confederation is spelled Piegan. Around 1900 the spelling was not yet standardized.

the Uhlenbeck household and thin air will have been found in the Uhlenbeck family's purse.

At the age of eighteen Uhlenbeck wrote a bundle of gloomy romantic poetry, titled *Gedachten en Droomen (Thoughts and Dreams)* but the reviews were not encouraging. Used to disappointments as he was, he went on and became a student at Leiden University. In 1891 he explained in a letter to Willem Jan van Eys (1825-1914), the first person in the Netherlands to study the Basque language that, when a student at University Leiden, he heard one of his professors argue that the Basque language had similarities with American-(Indian) languages. If this professor only could have known how his remark would steer Uhlenbeck for a great deal through life (as it does mine, words matter!).

In 1892 Uhlenbeck was appointed professor in the Sanskrit language in. In Amsterdam. From that year on he also published articles about the Basque languages. From 1899 he was professor of Old Germanic languages at University Leiden. That did not prevent him, from the years 1906 and 1907 on, to publish articles about Eskimo grammar and in 1908 an article about native languages in North-America. With regard to these languages, from 1909 on he restricted himself to Algonkin languages. In 1910 he published, in Dutch, the grammars of the Ojibway, Cree, Micmac, Natick and Blackfoot languages.[2] Meanwhile he was teaching Old Germanic languages.

On September 4, 1910 Uhlenbeck was back in Leiden, one month earlier than he had planned. To a colleague in Austria, Hugo Schuchardt (1842-1927), a scholar of the Basque language, he wrote that same day, September 4, that he had resided more than three months in the midst of the Southern Blackfoot Indians, adding that he had brought home much grammatical and ethnographical material and that it's processing might take several years. He ended this letter remarking that he believed to "have a sound basis for a scientific description of the Blackfoot language." This letter does not indicate that he intended to return to Montana, but that is what he did.

---

2. In 2013 this article is published in English translation by J. J. Snider as *Outline for a Comparative Grammar of Some Algonquian Languages: Ojibway, Cree, Micmac, Natick [Massachusett], and Blackfoot.*

Instead of staying home after his 1910 stay on the Blackfeet Reservation and publish a Blackfoot language grammar - what he only accomplished in 1938 - he was back at the Blackfeet in 1911, this time accompanied by his wife Willy Uhlenbeck-Melchior (1862-1954).

Uhlenbeck's work of the 1911 summer resulted in his 1912 *New Series of Blackfoot Texts*, which features a number of Napi stories, stories about lore, legends, life, death and adventure and also a number of stories, mostly by John Tatsey, that he classified as "Boys' Experiences." Uhlenbeck once in a while features in young Tatsey's stories about his daily activities as the "white man."

In the preface of *New Series of Blackfoot Texts,* Uhlenbeck noted about John's contributions to his work: "With only a few exceptions communicated and explained to me by my young friend John Tatsey, who also translated back into Blackfoot the portions from Bear-chief's life story, mentioned above."

In this book, *Blackfeet Tales & Teachings,* just the stories told by John Tatsey are presented, preceded by relevant entrees from Mrs. Uhlenbeck's diary.

Mrs. Uhlenbeck started her diary on the day of their arrival on the Blackfeet Reservation, which was on June 8, 1911. On June 11, she described a church service and John Tatsey being around that day. After a description of the breakfast enjoyed in the Tatsey tent; meeting staff of the Holy Family Mission, the Jesuit run boarding school at the reservation; the church service that day; meeting more people; entertaining mission boys in their tent and stories Bear Chief[3] and

John Tatsey, 1911.

---

3. Bear Chief, known as Young Bear Chief was 53 years old, full Piegan. His first wife was Fine Shield woman, full Piegan, children: Eddie Bear Chief 30 years, Medicine Pipe Woman,

Joe Tatsey[4] told her husband, Mrs. Uhlenbeck continued her diary on June 11:

> ... John comes in and lies down. They left about 10.00. [...] Later I also saw John & Joe Tatsey again on their horses beside their tent. [...]

On **June 12** Mrs. Uhlenbeck described the Tatsey children John's numerous siblings:

> ... I can now name Tatsey's children. They are Josephine, 21 years: she is not at home. For the time being we will not see her. Then Hattie follows - married to Charlie Guardipee, a very beautiful, slim young woman who is quite polite. However, she does not have that big friendliness like her mother, who is always busy and looks so friendly with her healthy, round face, her beautiful eyes and beautiful teeth. John, the oldest boy, 17 years old, looks like his mother. He is quiet and serious and has a beautiful face, a beautiful figure, though quite small. His leg injury from last year, which made him bedridden for weeks at home and later in a hospital outside the reservation, is completely cured. He never says much, in contrast to Joe - little Joe - who is next. A tough, wild, but cheerful, carefree boy who is always very nice to us. He always has something to say and races over the prairie on the wildest horses. Then Lizzy follows. She attends the mission school & will come home for holidays next week and then turns 12 years old. We haven't met her yet. Then follow Robert - or Bob - and Chubby, eight and six years old. Robert is the oldest of the two, but not the most handsome. However, he is the boy who is always with his grandmother and also sleeps in his grandmother's tent. Then Mary Louise follows, a shy, wild girl of five years old. Then George, a very nice young little Indian

---

Sebastian Bear Chief, Joseph Bear Chief. His second wife was Elk Yells in the Water, 44 years, ½ Blood, ½ Piegan: children were Lizzie Bear Chief, 11 years and Cecilia Bear Chief, 4 years. Bear Chief was once married to Medicine Shell. Child from that marriage is Petrified Rock, wife of Joseph still Smoking (DeMarce 1980: 287). As DeMarce mentions ages as they were in 1907/1908, in part I of this book I have added three years as the Uhlenbecks were in 1911 at the Blackfeet Reservation.

4. Joe or Joseph Tatsey, John's father, was ½ Blood, ¼ Piegan, 46 years (DeMarce 1980: 250).

of about three years old. He is very dark, has a round little face, with a nose that shall be a beautiful Indian nose in a couple of years. That peculiar line – that beautiful hook is already there. And he has red cheeks, pitch black eyes and hair that hangs untidy today, but yesterday was hanging from his head in small, short braids. I think that he is a most charming child to look at. He wears a light shirt that is tucked into his faded and half worn-out pants. The pants are too long for him and drag under his heels. That is just what makes him so cute. Cathie is the baby; she is well over one year old and is the youngest of Tatsey's ten children. Robert likes to elope once in a while to the Guardipees, which he did on Saturday night, [...][5]

Grandmother and Lizzy in 1911.

In *New Series of Blackfeet Tales,* the following is John's account of a church service at the Holy Family Mission. Uhlenbeck refers to it: "Boys' experiences, 20, communicated and explained to me by my young friend John Tatsey." All square brackets are part of the following texts. This story and the next ones are also in Uhlenbeck 1912: 225-245 and in Eggermont-Molenaar 2005.

20: Church

When they enter, they all kneel down and make the sign of the cross. They begin to pray. And then the priest enters, and he begins to pray. They

---

5. In 1912, Woodrow Tatsey would close the row of Tatsey children.
According to Wilma Adams, daughter of Hatty Guardipee, born in 1911, the Guardipees were Shoshones/Sioux (personal communication with Mrs. Adams in September 2002).

all sit down. And he begins to preach to them. And when he has done preaching, he kneels down again, and he sings, and the girls and the boys all sing. And he goes to sit down, and when the children have done singing, he gets up again, and the boys that serve at the altar get up, they take [the wine and water], that he drinks, and they bring them back, and they kneel down. And after a short while the priest preaches. One of the boys rings the bell, and the people are praying, they all kneel down, they bow their heads down. They ring the bell again. When they have rung the bell five times, then the people put their heads up. The priest preaches again. When he has done praying, the boys take again [the wine and water], that he drinks, and they put them away again. They go back and kneel down again. And they ring the bell again. When they have done ringing, they all sit down, and the priest comes down. He takes off the clothes, he uses while praying, and he puts on different [clothes]. He goes back again, he goes back up to the altar, and the girls and the boys sing again, and one of the boys is swinging the censer. He [the priest] gets up, he puts something in [the censer], then he goes up again, he takes down the Blessed Sacrament, he turns with it to the people, they bow their heads down again. When they have rung the bell again, they put their heads up, they sing again, and when they have done singing, the priest goes out. The people then all go out.

> **[Mrs. Uhlenbeck's diary notes] Monday June 19. ...** We are still busy getting dressed when Morning Eagle comes along again.[6] He is not yet allowed inside. We first go for a quick breakfast with *hot cakes* and now the ancient man (now on foot with a cane) comes for a little while into our tent. Even so, Uhlenbeck starts working with John. First I am writing outside. But it starts to get windy and I have to go inside because otherwise my papers will blow away. John again reports how he spends his day. He lies on our camp bed & once in a while is sleepy. [...]

---

6. According to Fuller (1898: 71), Morning Eagle was at that time 65-years old, married to Catches On Top (32-years) and Hits On Top (40-years) and he had two sons, John (7), George (4) and one daughter, Two Rabbits (2). Source: internet. Morning Eagle, "no age," had eight wives of whom five had died (DeMarce 1980: 249).

Uhlenbeck refers to the following stories as to: "Boys' experiences, 1-5, 7 and 9, communicated and explained to me by my young friend John Tatsey."

1: Friday in the morning I got up at five o'clock. I built a fire, I took my hat and my coat. I walked to [the place], where I had tied my horse. I cut him loose, I brought him home, I put the saddle on him. I then walked in, I put wood on the stove. Then I went out again, I got on my horse, I went out on horseback. I drove the cattle out [of the corral]. And when they began to eat, I went up to a rock. I got off my horse, I sat down [on the rock], I looked round down from there. Men on horseback were running all over, they looked for their horses. And after a while I walked down, I drove our horses, I drove them home. We cut [two] work-horses loose, we put the harness on them. And I walked in. I began to eat. I went out again, I got in the wagon, I drove down, I loaded up some meat. I went back, I took an axe and a knife and a book. Then I started out again. I began to cut the meat, I was selling it, and they finally bought it all. I then went back down, I took the harness off the horses, I entered. I began to count the money I got [for the beef], there were forty dollars. I then put the harness on the horse, I went on horseback, and I was running around about Birch creek [looking for horses], and it looks very fine [over there]. But I did not stay there very long. I then went back, and they [all the fellows] were working on the ditch. I then came back. They had all stopped [working]. I then took the harness off the horses. I entered, I went out again, I went to the river. And I talked with my elder sister. She then walked away. She told me: Come up [to my camp] after a while. I entered [my own camp], I ate [supper]. When I had done eating, I then went to those white men.[7] I then went to them there, and there was a lot of people, I then walked over to them. And it was dark. I came back again, and I then entered my brother-in-law's camp. He was playing violin. Then I went back to my own camp. I then entered, and all were asleep. I then went to bed, I went to sleep again.

---

7. Not sure which white men these men were; Uhlenbeck and Grinnell?

2: Sunday in the morning I got up, I went after the horses, I got in [the camp] with the horses. I got a saddle-horse, I just put the saddle on him. I rode higher up, I walked around. I came back again, I went to tie up my horses, I changed saddle-horses. I then started out to Birch creek. I went there, I chased the cattle, [and] the horses. And after a while I came back again to a house. I then went in. And after a while there was a rider coming, he was driving horses. He drove them into the corral, he caught them and brought them out. I myself went in [into the corral], I began to rope the horses. After I got through roping, I drove them out. I got on my horse. We rode over to a cow, we then drove it, we ran it up [the road]. We got quite a way out, it would not go straight. I roped it round the neck. And the other boy roped it round the leg. We threw it down. Then it got up again. We started it out again. We got quite a way out again, it was tired. Then we left it. And I roped there also another one. We threw it also down. I tied its legs up. And [the other boy's] horse stepped into the rope. He [that horse] then ran around, he broke the rope, he then ran away. I caught him. I nearly died from laughing. We then went back to [the place], where the cow was lying, and one rope was loose, and the other one was just about to come off. And that boy got off [his horse]. He was going to give me the rope. And [the other rope] came off. I chased it again, we roped it again, we then sat by it. We rolled a cigarette, we did not have any matches, we were looking for some. I found one. We then went [on horseback] to a house. We entered, we built a fire, and so we got to light our cigarettes. Then we smoked. And when I had got through smoking, we went again [on horseback]. We then came to Blackfoot creek, we walked around [on horseback] in the water. It was getting late, we started again this way. And we got here. I turned my horse loose. Then I went in. Then I ate. When I was through eating, I walked out. And I entered this [other] tent here. I talked with that white man, he was telling me stories about the dance [in the afternoon], how it had been.[8] And after a short while

---

8. It could have been the Sunday of June 18, 1911. That day the Uhlenbecks had attended the Beaver Dance; according to Mrs. Uhlenbeck's diary only at 10 p.m. "all the visitors' were gone."

I went out. I walked up, and I entered a tent, and there were people sitting in it. I sat by one of them, I then was talking with him. And it was dark, I then went home, and they had gone all to bed. I went to bed myself. And there ended my running around, [that had begun] on Sunday-morning.

3: After I had got through teaching, I went. And there I was nailing the tongue of a wagon. And when I got through nailing it, I went in, that I might eat. Then I ate. When I had done eating, then I went out again. I began to nail it [the tongue] again. After I was through nailing it, I was tying it. When I had done tying it, I went in again. I then took a certain piece of paper. Then I went to my brother-in-law's tent. Then I went in. I then gave him that piece of paper. He was looking at it. When he had done looking, then he gave me some money. I then went to the store. Then I went in. I asked a man: Is there any butter? He said: There is none. I asked him again: Are there any fruit-cans? And he said: There are none. And I told him: [Give me] one package of matches. And he gave them then to me. Then I went out. Then I went over to the blacksmith's shop. I sat behind it. And after a short while there a boy came along, he told me: Help me for a while to hook up my team. Then I helped him. When I had done helping him, we got in [into the wagon]. Then we went higher up. We left the wagon. Then we went down [afoot]. And there was another wagon, we hooked up our team to that one. Then I came to my camp. I got to it. I took water, I poured it out on my head. And here I entered. I began to tell you stories about what I had done, which you wrote down. And that is all.

4: Sunday in the morning I got up. I went to catch a horse, I went to Medicine-wolf's house. There I found my horses. I drove them. When I had driven them back to camp, I caught some of them. After I had put the harness on them, I tied them up. I saddled up, I got on my horse, I went to my brother-in-law's tent. I came there, I went in, I stayed there and some other boys came there. And some girls rode [on our horses]. And after a while they [these girls] went back. I caught my horse. I then went to our horses, I drove them, I drove them again to camp. I then tied up my horse, I went home. I turned my saddle-horse loose. Then I went to my brother-in-law's tent, I then went again, I caught his horses, I put the harness on them. Then I went with the wagon across [the creek]. They butchered. Then we came back, we sold the meat. About ten o'clock it was very dark. I turned the horses loose. I went in, I stayed there a while. We ate. When we had done eating, I went home. When I came home, I looked at the clock. It was already twelve o'clock. I then went to bed. In the morning I got up about seven o' clock. I got up, then I went again to my brother-in-law's tent. I got there again, I ate breakfast there. When I had done eating, then I went to catch his horses. After I had put the harness on them, I went with the wagon higher up. I stopped then, and women began to buy the meat. One of them said: Cut it right here. So I cut it there, and she was looking at it. She said: I will not take it. I told her: I never told you, that you should take it. If I think, that I shall not give you any, [then] I shall not give you any. And after a while she came back. She said: Give me some. I then left them. Then I went back, and I got here.

5: I saw Willy yesterday,9 I just greeted him, [but] I did not talk with him. I then went again to Bearchief's house, I got there. When I had done eating, I told Sebastian: Come with me. Then we went, we got there [at Seville]. We left the meat. Then we went back again, and we got to a lake. It then began

Willy Kennedy 1911.

---

9. This was 12-year old Willy Kennedy. After *Montana 1911: A Professor and his Wife among the Blackfeet* was published in 2005, Willy's second son, Charles Kennedy contacted me (2007). He told me that in 1924 Uhlenbeck had taken up correspondence with his father Willy and that seven of Uhlenbecks's letters were found in the basement of his older brother. In one of these letters Uhlenbeck wrote that he had been planning take Willy along to the Netherlands and give him an education. It did not happen. Uhlenbeck's interest in young Willy might also explain that he returned to the Blackfeet and, that John Tatsey bothers to mention that "he saw Willy."

to rain, it rained hard. Then we went slowly. We finally got back home [at Bear-chief's]. I then went straight on up to the bridge. Then I slept. And in the morning, I started again, and I got here. I then began to walk around.

7: [How I lived "up the round".] Then we started at the bridge and [went over] to the Old Agency. We ate dinner there. And then we went to Birch creek. I then caught a black horse. We went over to eat something. There is the house of a partner of mine. We went there to eat. When we were through eating, then we started out again, and we got over there to Fish's springs. And in the morning, we caught horses, we all rode out then. I was the last one, I kicked the horse I rode, he began to buck with me, I was about to fall off. He stopped bucking. We were running then. And there might be about seven hundred head of cattle. We began to cut out [the strays] [from the cattle] that we drove. And we began to brand the calves. When we got through, we went home to the camp. We turned the horses loose, then we ate. And in the morning at four o'clock we got up, and then we rode out again. We drove back again, we went home to eat. When we had done eating, we caught some more horses. When we got through working, then we went back to camp. When we got there, two horses ran off. I chased them. The horse I rode began to buck with me again. I then turned him loose. In the morning we moved camp, and we camped there at the Old Agency. In the afternoon I again took that bay horse, I got on him, he was bucking again. And my father came, he was whipping the horse I rode. Then we ran out. And it rained. We had done working then, we went home. In the morning we moved camp again. We then camped near Owl-child's lake. We had done working. And in the morning we rode out to Black-tail creek. We were branding again. At two o'clock we went home. And in the morning we moved camp to Heart butte. We camped there. And when we had done working, we moved camp again, and [now] to Badger creek. Where the ditch comes out [of Badger creek], there we camped. And next morning we again moved camp, and [now] to Little Badger creek. And we stayed there two days, [and] then it snowed, and I then went home. I went to the Mission.

And [when] I had stayed there three days, then I went to White-calf's hay-ground,[10] and they were camped there already. And after two days we moved camp again. And then we camped near the old bull-corral. Then we gathered all the cattle up. And next morning we moved camp again. Near Dancer's home on the other side of the hill, there was a lake. We camped there. And there were a few boys, with whom [literally: with them] I went. There were some cows, we were going to drive them. We drove them far, we were going to rope them. And myself, I roped a steer, that was going there, round its horns. And then my rope got tangled up on my saddle. That steer ran away, I then fell off, it kicked me. I got a hold of him. And he ran over me. We then went back, we moved camp, and we camped near the ditch-workers. And in the morning we moved camp again. And then we camped by a spring. I was watching some cows, [that] there were. I went to sleep, and it might be about one hour, that I was sleeping. I woke up, I went home to the camp, I ate, I stayed there then. And in the morning we moved camp again, and we camped in a deep coulee, where they cut hay. And in the morning we moved camp again. We then camped near New-woman's husband's lake. Next morning we moved camp again. And then we camped way up near the old station over there. And in the morning we moved camp again, and we camped then near Browning [literally: Creek]. And we did not stay there very long. We moved camp again. Then we camped near Kipp's springs. And next day in the afternoon

Holy Family Mission, schoolhouse and church around 1911.

---

10. White Calf is known to be the last chief of the Piegan. In 1903 he died when in Washington, arguing sales of Blackfeet territory, see this add in the *New York Times* of January 30, 1903: query.nytimes.com/mem/archive-free/pdf?res=9E0DE3D7143BE430A75752C3A96 79C946297D6CF (last consulted in June 2018).

we quit working. My father [and myself] then went home. And that is all.

9: [How I go trapping.] In the afternoon I am going. I take my traps and a cow-head, I carry them along. And when I have gone quite a way off, then I put the head down, and I put the traps around it. I stake them. Then I go back, I take some fish, I go and get another pair of traps. Then I come to the river. I put the traps. Then I go home. And in the morning I go to my traps. I go there, and there will be a kit-fox. And then I go over to my other trap. I then get to it also, I then have trapped a mink too. One week, I was trapping, I sent twelve [skins], that I had caught by trapping, down [to Minneapolis]. I got fifteen dollars for them.

[Mrs. Uhlenbeck's diary notes]
Tuesday June 20:
Again we have breakfast together. It will be nice when Tatsey is home again. I think that he will only be coming on Wednesday, because, coming from Browning he might go first to *Birch*, to his *log house*. U. works the whole morning again with John: 1½ notebooks already filled by teacher John! Jimmy Vielle,[11] a mission kid, tells "a story about a day at the *mission school*." That

Joe and Annie Tatsey, 1911.

---

11. James Vielle, 13-years old, was the son of Frank Vielle, 44 years, ½ Piegan, and Susan The Hoofs Vielle, 46-years, full Piegan (DeMarce 1980: 264).

is nice & so Jimmy keeps John awake [...]. John's teaching continues again.

Friday June 23
The weather is fine. Not warm & lots of clouds. I take a picture of John, of John with U. & of the three little ones, Bob, Chub & George, + Bobbie stands there each time has his fingers in his mouth. George wants to turn around each time. Still it succeeds because John helps a bit. [...] Uhlenbeck & John are quietly working - body parts of the cow - and once in a while they talk about several boys and about the killing of animals. [...] Tatsey is still not back. But we get somewhat used to his absence. John progresses in the right direction but still I long to see *the old man,* that is Tatsey, come back.

John's teachings are in Uhlenbeck's article "*A Survey of the Non-Pronominal and Non-Formative Affixes of the Blackfoot Verb,*" on the pages 101 and 120. This article was only published in 1920. In its preface Uhlenbeck thanks "the regretted Joseph Tatsey and his son John."

p. 101: -*pisak*—hind-part, thigh, cf. *oápisàkists*—its hind-quarters (e.g. of a cow). *itaitapisakiu*—he would hold his hind-part to (the side from where the wind blew) (in nbt. 176). *akaiitapisak-sitòkaie*—he then was suddenly shot by him (4 p.) in the thigh, so that there was a gap in it (in nbt. 183).

p. 120: hind-part (his) *oómoχtotsopop* ("his where-we-sit-on")—the

John Tatsey with Uhlenbeck, 1911.

hindquarters of a cow and other quadrupeds are called *oápisàkists*. Cf. *-pisak-*, and thing, upper leg.

> **[Mrs. Uhlenbeck's diary notes]**
> **Saturday June 24: First cold afternoon:** I rise at 7:30. The thermometer reads 50°; it is really cold & it is windy & raining hard. About ten o'clock the weather gets nice and I take a picture of Uhlenbeck with John again – because the previous evening I developed the one of *John* too early in the evening. John alone & Peter & Mary Bear Leggings.[12]
>
> When Joe leaves at eleven for Browning to pick up his father who seems to have arrived in Browning, he takes with him my letters to Mama & the sisters. The weather is deteriorating again fast. The wind picks up again, it also starts to rain hard & the temperature drops again. In the morning Uhlenbeck does not work with John. John is suffering a *belly-ache* & would rather stroll around & chat. And John promises to write to us later on a regular basis. While it is raining hard, we eat.

Peter and Mary Bear Legging 1911.

---

12. Mary Bear Leggings, 10-years, was a daughter, and Peter Bear Leggings, 13-years old was a son of Charging Home and Stephen Henault. Charging Home had Peter and Mary with her first husband Bear Leggings, deceased (DeMarce 1980: 127).

John spends the whole afternoon in our tent. The thermometer sinks to 40° & stays that low. Late that evening it is 42°. And it does not go higher. It is most unpleasantly cold in the tent. It is blowing in from all sides around us & at the side of the suitcases a lot of water enters the tent. I pull the suitcases towards me & put thick sticks underneath. U. is so cold in the afternoon that he crawls into his bed at 3.00 with big, thick night socks. John is going to sit at the foot end on his feet to warm them, but this does not help much either. I use the meths burner for the first time, & for warmth and to stay cozy the three of us drink bouillon. It is blowing so hard that Uhlenbeck can hardly hear John, even though they sit next to each other. It is a cold, unpleasant afternoon, but our mood is very good. John is so nice and relates in Peigan everything about his leg injury of last year. We both get along very well with John. At the end of the afternoon Uhlenbeck tells him a brief account of the *Karamasows*. John listens attentively, also to the introduction of *The thousand and one nights*. Later I would like to get a good English translation of the *1001 nights*. U. would love to send this to John later.

At 6:00 we pick up our evening meal. U. is not yet warmed up & I give him a sip of rum. I wrap myself in my raincoat & John closes our tent behind me. From tent to tent there is nothing but puddles. In Tatsey's tent it is warm & cozy; all the children are inside.

The stories John Tatsey told on June 24 are in *"Boys' experiences,"* no's. 11,12 and 13.

11: [How I make fire.] I then make shavings, I light them. And I put small pieces of wood on top [of the shavings]. Then it burns.

12: How my mother bakes bread. She then takes flour, and she puts it in her pan. And [also] salt and baking-powder. And she puts water in [the pan]. She begins to knead it, and she puts it in [the stove]. And when it is done, she takes it out [of the stove], and we eat it. And that is all.

13: My sickness. The first time, that my leg pained, we went over to our ranch. And when we got back, then next morning we went over to Blackfoot station. We went back then. When we got home, I went to bed. And in the morning I tried to get up. I could not get up. I looked at my leg, and it was swollen. They were doctoring me. And about one week it mattered. They opened it. It was one day and a half, that the matter was running. And I could not sleep at all from it. During one month it pained. And it stopped. And it was another month, that I did not get up. In the first part of Christmas-month [i.e. December] I got up. The first thing I then did was to ride, I went to the Mission, I got there, I came back. We then moved up to the bridge, we camped there. Next morning we moved back down again. We then camped by the Mission. In [the month] When-the geese-come [i.e. March] we moved over to our ranch. One month we stayed at home. We then moved back [to Two-Medicine river].

We camped by Bad-John's house. The third day of this last month they brought me away to Conrad [literally: Where-they-used-to-freight-the-flour-from]. Then they brought me there. It was three months, that I stayed there. In [the first part of] haying-time [i.e. the beginning of August] I came back home, and then I have seen you. I did not know you, when my father told me your name. In the afternoon I saw you there at the door, I was standing there, you came in, and you asked my father: Is that one another boy of yours? He told you: Yes. You came up to me, you shook hands with me. About two weeks [afterwards] you went away. I then felt lonesome for you, that you went away. And that is all.

Monday July 2: ... Near Mountain Chief's tipi a *Crow dance* is in progress. [13] We watch it for a long time. It is too crowded to get in. Around the tipi it is also crowded with spectators. [...]

Monday in the evening they began to drum. The people here thought, the Grass dancers might be dancing.[14] There were a great many people [singing in a tent]. The man, who owned the tent, said: Sing four [songs] more, that you may quit then. And [when] their four songs were finished, they separated.

---

13. A Crow dance is generally held "on Sundays and at the time of the new moon. Everybody may look in, but only members [of the Crow-Water Society] can come inside of the tipi or ceremonial circle" (Wissler 1913: 437, citing Iron, founder of this society).
14. The Grass Dances were held over the next days, the 4th and the 5th of July.

Aug. 5: ... We have trout for breakfast, a delicious change from the leathery steaks! [...]

One of these days, John Tatsey must have told Uhlenbeck "How I go fishing." *Boys' experiences*, nr.10, nsbt, 236-37 and Eggermont-Molenaar (2005: 316).

> **10 [How I go fishing.]** I then go, I then take my fish-pole. Then I get to the river. I throw my fish-line in [into the water]. I then walk down to [a place], where it is deep. I fish there. I catch about two. I go farther on, I begin to fish again. When I am long ways off, then my grass-hoppers are all gone. I begin to catch some. When I have caught quite a few grass-hoppers, I go back to the river. I begin to fish again, and there are lots of fish, and they are wild, and I don't catch a great many, just about ten. It may be, I catch more of them. I get tired, then go back, I will finally get home. When I get home, I clean the fish. And when we go to eat, I take flour, and I put the fish into it. I put the frying-pan on the fire. And I put some grease in the frying-pan. And when it [the pan] is hot, I put the fish in the frying-pan. And when they are all cooked, we eat them. And when we have done eating, I get pretty full. And now the boiling is ended [that means: the story is at an end].

Tatsey & son were these days very possibly translating "From Bearchief's life story" back into Blackfoot. Bear Chief told his story to Uhlenbeck in 1910. It is published in *Original Blackfoot Texts* (69-91).

> **August 28 and September 5 and 9:** ... Tatsey works until twelve thirty with Uhlenbeck. John dropped in for a moment & will come and *teach* at 2:00 for one more hour for a halve dollar. However, John only comes at 2:30 and thinks that he is right on time. He was fishing with Joe & Jim White Man.[15] He cheerfully chats & again Uhlenbeck and I come under his spell. *Teaching* progresses *slow*. John finds it difficult. He will receive his personal fee at the end of the week. John likes that better, too & also Uhlenbeck would not have that much change, because we are very thrifty with it. His visit broke up the long afternoon a bit. [...]

---

15. Jim or James White Man was a son of Whiteman and sixth wife, Pine Needles Woman (DeMarce 1980: 275).

September 5: [...] I worked a lot on my diary. At 3:00 John Tatsey comes and stays until 5:00. That is nice. Uhlenbeck pays him three dollars for teaching and two dollars as a present. Tatsey likes that. He doesn't say thanks but the young Indian flushes & that clearly indicates his inner emotion. He is very nice & breaks up the time for us a lot, but again he has no whiskey.

September 9: [...] Uhlenbeck works in the tent with John, who is sleepy & hungry. He did not get dinner. He will go first and eat something at his mother's. Our last two biscuits, from the time we were snow-bound, and a few sweets aren't enough for him. He leaves & indeed comes back 10 to 15 minutes later. Now they work again. I believe they deal with *Bear Chief's life story*. Now *from* English *into* Peigan. After John has left, we go again quickly to the Cree valley & have our evening meal there. Everything is orderly & and nice again [...]

Bear Chief around 1900-1905.

This translation is in *New Series of Blackfoot Texts* (211-214) and in Eggermont-Molenaar (2005: 339-340).

From Bear-chief's life-story.
"Translated from English into Blackfoot by John Tatsey."
1. Mátsistapakàuo ksistsikuísts nitsikóputsi souíiks. Nínoχkyàio ítomo. Kepitápii nitsítapìkoaiks ki túkskαma anáukitapìkoan. Sauumáitautoχsau Pinápisinai otáuaχsini, itsíppiainoyìau nátsitapìi iχ̇kitópii itápoχkitòpii atsóàskui niétαχtai. Itákàuyiau, ki omíksi iχ̇kitópiks itsinísuiauanìau, ki itsístsàpiksiau. Omíksi Pekánikoaiks itsinóyiauaiks, otsápikoanasaiks, ki itanístsiau omí anáukitapìkoan, máχksiniχ̇kαtαχsaiks, máχksàkapuχsaiks, máχkstaiskunαksau, Pekάniua óksòkoa nápikoaiks. Otáisakapuχsau, omíksi Pekánikoaiks itunnóyiau, otsikétaiisksimàniaiks. Itsópoaχtsìsatsìiau omíksi nápikoaiks, otáitapoχpiaiks. Itaníau: Pinápisinaua nitáχpummokinàna nápiáχkèists. Omá anáukitapìkoan itanístsiu omíksi nápikoaiks: Toχkókinoàiniki kisókàsoaists, nitákoχpokiuo, kitákitspummòχpuau. Itoχkótsiauaie asókàsi, ki omá anáukitapìkoan itanístsiu omíksi Pekánikoaiks: Ánnòmάkaitùpik, áikòkus istákaipiskoχtòk amóm Pinápisinàu, ákoχtαtsèiua nápiáχke. Áipstsikisàmo itáistoχkim akékànists, ki itóχtoyìau Pinápisinài otáiistsèkinsaie, ki sotámisksinoyìauaie, otauátsisaie. Nínoχkyàio itsinóyiu omí nitsítapìkoan, áiisksipistsènyai ótàs, istáiinyài, máχkαtoχkòtαksiaie nápiáχke. Nínoχkyàio kámosatsìu omím ponokámitai, ki otoχpokómiks iχ̇tsítokòyi amóistsi moyísts, okámosoaiks ponoka'mitaiks niíppi piχ̇ksékopùtsi. Sotαmomatòiau, itsítskitsìau omí anáukitapìkoan omístsim Pinápisinàuyists. Omá anáukitapìkoan itsitsítsiuaiks, ki itanístsiuaiks: Omám Pinápisinànαm iχ̇púmmau nápiáχke ponokámitaiks ki imoiániks. Itoχpókiuòiau omíksisk nápikoaiksk ki omí anáukiapìkoan, áutoimìanaiks, omoχtátsαχsau nisíppiks ótàsoàuaiks. Itótomoyiauaiks omíksim ponokámitaiks, ki itáuauaχkautsèiau. Túkskαma omíksi nápikoaiks itóau oχkátsi. Omíksi Pekánikoaiks sotαmoχtaχkàiiau.

From Bear-chief's life-story

1. A few days after that there were eleven in a war-party. There were ten full-bloods and one half-breed. Before they got to the Sioux country, they saw from a distance two riders, who rode towards the timber on the river. They charged, and then the riders jumped off their horses, and fled into the brush. The Peigans saw, that they were white men, and said to the half-breed, that he should call to them to come out [and] not to shoot at them, because the Peigans were friends of the white men. When they came out, the Peigans saw, that they had pack-horses. They asked the white men, where they were going. They said: We are trading whiskey to the Sioux. The half-breed told the white men: If you give me some of your clothes, I shall go with you, I shall help you trade. They gave him some clothes, and then the half-breed told the Peigans: Stay here for a while, make a raid on the Sioux in the night, they will be drunk from the whiskey. After a short while they got near the camp, and they heard the Sioux making noise, and then they knew, that they were drunk. Bear-chief saw an Indian, who was tying his horse, wishing to get some more whiskey. Bear-chief stole that horse, and his companions went through the camp, stealing 39 horses. Then they started off, they left the half-breed in the Sioux camp. The half-breed overtook them, and told them: the Sioux have bought whiskey for horses and robes. They went after the white men and the half-breed, blaming them, because they had lost 40 head of their horses. They took those horses from them, and they had a fight. One of the white men was shot in his leg. The Peigans then returned home.
 [Cf. Uhlenbeck obt 76 sq]

From Bear-chief's life-story.
Translated from English into Blackfoot by John Tatsey.
2. Mátsipuχsapakauò ksistskíusts mátsitsitàkomatopò
Nínoχkyàyio. Nisúitapìi Pekánikoaiks ki iχkitsíkippitapìi
Isapóiikoaiks. Pinàpisinài áukakiosatsìau okaχtómoai, ki
itsiníyianaiks otáistauauaχkàniaiks. Itákaàtseiau
Nínoχkyàyo ki otoχpokómiksai. Omíksi Isapóiikoaiks
iikákimàiau, ki itsinóyianaiks otáistauanaχkàniaks. Itákaàtseiau
Nínoχkyàyoi ki otoχpokómiksai. Omíksi Isapóiikoaiks iikákimàiau,
máχkotsimmotàniau. Nínoχkyàyo ki omíksi matsóksaipekànikoaiks
anatóχtsik iχtóiau ki áuaχkautsìmiau Pinápisinài.
Autamátíχtàtsikaiksistsiku otsítsaipiskoχtòk Pinápisinài, ki
áiikotàko itsíkyaiaiksitauaχkautsèiau. Sotámaχkàiiau ánni
atákuyi, ki paiánnauatòiau. Ksiskaniáutuniì Nínoχkyàioa itsínikiu
skéini. Itsîìtsiauki sotámomatàpioyiau. Otsákiauyisau, itsinóyiau
omí iχkitópi itótamiaipuyìnai omí ákiksaχkuyi. Itsítsipsatsiu
Nínoχkyàyoi otsitapímiks, ki áχkaukaksepuyìau nátsitapìi
stámsokatsitotsi puχpaipìii, ki ítskunakatsìau Nínoχkyàyoi
otoχpóksìmiks. Otáinoaχsauaiks, otákaitapìsaiks, itsístapukskàsiau.
Pinápisinaikoaniiaiks. Omíksi Isapóiikoaiks iχpókiuòiau omíksisk
Pinápisinaikoaiks. Nínoχkyàioa ki omíksi stsíkiks misksíppotapòiau,
ki itsinóyiau iχkitópi Pinápisinaikoàninai. Omà iχkitópiuai
istsíppiksiu. Omíksi stsíkiks mátskàkspummoyìuaiksauaie,
ki Nínoχkyàio nitisitápiiu iχtsápoaie, ki ánistsinoàsai
áiskunχkχtsìmaie, otáisàkapipiks omá Pinápisinaikoan,
itsauátoχkotoχtoàtau. Nínoχkyàio itsitápoχtoχpàtskimauaie, ki
omá Pinápisinaikoan itâskunakatsìuaie, ki Nínoχkyàio ótàs
saiékatsìuaie onámai. Stámipotoyìn omá Pinápisinaikoan. Omá
ponokámita itapóχpatskuyinaie. Stámipuau omám Pinápisinaikoan
itótoyiu onámai. Nátokyaiaskùnakatsiu Níχoχkyàio, ki
ómoχtsokskaχpi onámaiitsáuatoχkotoχtskùnakin. Nínoxkyàio
iχtsítoχtauàtsiuaie ómaχksistoàninai, ki soksipískskiuaie,
ki imatátsistsinimaie úskitsipaχpi, ki itsíkaχkokitsìuaie,
otsauumáinisaie. Isapóiikoaiks itaχká nauto iχ kitsíkippitapìi.
Nitúyi Nínoχkyàioa otoχpokómiks niuókskaitapìi itoχkítaipuyìau
omí nitúmmoi, ki itótakìau nánisoyimi ótàsiks omím
Pinápisinaikoanim, ómam áitskamiu Nínoχkyàioi. Auauatóiau
kokúsi ki ksistsikús, máχkotaχkàiisau.

From Bear-chief's life story

2. A few days later Bear-chief started on a new trip. There were four Peigans and seventy Crows. The Sioux were looking out for enemies, and saw the war-party coming. Then they made a charge on Bear-chief and his companions. The Crows did their very best to escape. Bear-chief and the three other Peigans stayed behind and fought the Sioux. It was about noon, [when] the Sioux made a charge on them, and it was late in the evening, before they stopped fighting. They then started home that evening, and travelled all night. Early in the morning Bear-chief killed a buffalo-cow. They skinned it and then they commenced to eat. Whilst they were eating still, they saw a rider, standing on a high bank, just above them. He spoke to Bear-chief's people, and before they could answer, two more jumped up at his side and shot at Bear-chief's companions. [But] when they saw, that there were so many, they ran away. They were Sioux. The Crows went after those Sioux. Bear-chief and the [three] others went in the opposite direction, and saw there a rider, a Sioux. That rider fled into the brushes. The others did not want to help him, but Bear-chief alone followed him, and shot at him, every time he saw him through the brush, till the Sioux went out on the prairie, [and] then he was hard to get at. Bear-chief rode up to him, and the Sioux would shoot him, but Bear-chief's horse kicked his gun. Then the Sioux let it loose. The horse then ran over him. Then the Sioux got up, [and] took his gun. He shot at Bear-chief twice, but the third time his gun refused to work. Then Bear-chief attacked him with a butcher-knife, and cut him over his face, and stabbed him near his heart, and cut off his head, before he died. Then the Crows, the whole seventy, came up. At the same time Bear-chief's three companions were standing on a hill and took eight horses from the Sioux, who was fighting Bear-chief. They travelled night and day to get home.
[Cf. UHLENBECK obt 79].

On 17 September, 1911, the Uhlenbecks returned home, to their house along the Rhine River in the city of Leiden, the Netherlands. The horse and buggy trip from their abode to the Browning railway station gave some ado, also because of the weather, but finally they were on their way. The last thing we hear about John in Mrs. Uhlenbeck's diary foreshadows so to speak his later occupation:

Nieuwe Rijn 69, Leiden, 2015.

Sunday September 17: Up at 6:30. I still have to rummage around a lot. At 8:00 Uhlenbeck is at Tatsey's, before I am. I also first close the second large suitcase and tie the rope around it. Everything is completely ready when I go to Tatsey's at 8:30. Uhlenbeck had already had his lonely breakfast; I also eat something quickly. It will be one more hour before we can leave. The weather is too cold for the old aunt & the sister. They will not leave today. Then Tatsey wants to give us *a light wagon* & no *buggy* & also loads the suitcases onto it, & "John," he says, "will drive you & sit in front of you & bring you along like that & so I save a second *team*." However, Uhlenbeck is very dissatisfied and when Tatsey notices that this discourse is not to our liking, he says, *"Now, Professor, you shall have it."* We ask Tatsey's wife for the food for the road. She doesn't know anything about it and keeps her finger in her mouth, looking shy. It doesn't matter. We can do without it and try to get something later, in Browning.

Joe is asking whether we can come to our own tent to give instructions for the large suitcases. That means walking up & down and it is raining continuously. Joe First One unties the suitcase rope from the tent pole and brings it inside to me.[16] Sometimes it rains hard. We can see less and less of the Rockies. It will be a bad day. We return to Tatsey's camp where we will mount the borrowed big *buggy*. There we will be wrapped up well from the rain. Joe First One is there again. *"Behave yourself, Joe, and be a good boy,"* and Uhlenbeck firmly shakes our mission friend's hand.

Adam also comes to say goodbye. He greets us by our Indian names. For the last time spoken by an Indian mouth. *Omachksistamik* and *Sakoo ake!* It resonates deeply in my soul! Uhlenbeck speaks for one more moment to Adam & sends greetings to the old man. David also comes. We hear that Camil broke his leg. And now we have to say goodbye to all of the Tatseys, big and small. Tatsey has his head bent and doesn't look cheerful. He won't take us himself. But John will be our driver and Joe will take the wagon with the suitcases.

I am the first to mount the high *buggy* and then Tatsey comes to wrap me with coverings, coats and blankets. I can barely move. Uhlenbeck will sit in the front beside John and among other things he gets Tatsey's fur coat around him. Adam still says: "Please blanket Sakoo-aki very well."[17] Everything is ready. We say goodbye and look at them time and again and we drive away on this chilly, wet, fall morning. We leave the Cree valley going along the back of the tent and past the *store*. We get to the Badger through a detour. We have to cross it. Water is splashing on all sides; the stream is very strong, and the bottom

---

16. Joe First One, 11-years, was the son of First One Russel and Isabelle (DeMarce 1980: 223).
17. "Sakoo-Akè" is how Willy spelled "Sakóàke," the name given to her. Uhlenbeck and Van Gulik (1934: 329): *Sakóàke* (-àkeua) an. *Last-woman*, a certain white woman's Indian name, obv. -àke (i). Geers (1917, 110): "Sako - last. 1° as an element of nominal forms: Sakóàke *Last-woman* (name given to Mrs. Uhlenbeck)." Uhlenbeck (1938: 65): "Sakóàke *Last-woman* (a woman's name) (: àké woman)."

here is also very rocky. Then we ride over the high prairie hills, through deep valleys. The road is extremely bad, the weather extremely unpleasant. The sky is dismal and there will be rain and wind until the end of the ride. But John is nice and that is why the cold and all the wetness don't get to us that much. John tells a lot about his life as a boy on the prairie, his young life full of unrest and harassment. Uhlenbeck listens very attentively to him and I quietly wonder time and again about John's open-heartedness.

We have to cross Two Medicine River again, but now we take the bridge. Then the road sometimes gets really bad and really slippery; time and again the horses slip, but John doesn't think it necessary to dismount. He knows his horses so well and he is a good driver. Once in a while we look back at Joe, who follows us, sometimes right behind, then further back. A bit further past Two Medicine we see Green Grass Bull near his *log cabin*. His adopted brother wants to ride along with Joe. He says a few Indian words to Uhlenbeck and for the last time we hear a lively *discours* in Peigan, between him and John.

We left at 9:30, now, about 2:00, we approach the depot, the Browning station. First we pass the rail line. You drive towards it along a slanted slope, going slowly, and we keep looking out to see whether an express train might approach at high speed. Then it even hails, coming down hard on us. The horses want to turn aside, they turn their heads away from the wind and John has to turn to the side and stop. "*It hurts my face*," he says, as if for us it is just a pleasure to drive in this weather over the open plain. There is the *depot*. We dismount, cold and stiff. The suitcases are loaded off, checked in against receipts and Uhlenbeck takes out the tickets for us, too. There is a problem. The chief doesn't have tickets for New York in stock. In the meantime I warm myself at the big stove burning inside and then we go with the boys to the *section house* that belongs to the *depot* five minutes further along. There we eat together. There, at Mrs. Clifford's, it is so nice & warm and then the two brothers leave. At least Joe, who is always scared of ghosts, wants to be back home before dark. "In a week," says John, "I will write." We say goodbye and

> Uhlenbeck watches them for a long time; for a long time he watches Johnny and thinks, *"I like that feller!"* And we, for hours and hours we sit near the warm stove. The express train comes at 10:19. The bright light approaches rapidly, the train stops, the *negro* is ready with his steps, we get in and suddenly we are in the Pullman Car. There is no wind around me, no rain either, but our Indians aren't there anymore. Prairie life belongs to the past.

It took Mrs. Uhlenbeck only a few days to name and describe all the Tatsey kids. Remember what she wrote about John on July 12, 1911:

> John, the oldest boy, 17 years old, looks like his mother. He is quiet and serious and has a beautiful face, a beautiful figure, though quite small. His leg injury from last year, which made him bedridden for weeks at home and later in a hospital outside the reservation, is completely cured. He never says much, in contrast to Joe - *little Joe* - who is next.

Mrs. Uhlenbeck's description very much fits the John Tatsey that emerges in her diary. From John's own accounts about his own "boys' experiences," looking for horses, chasing cattle, branding calves, building fires, cutting wood and repairing wagons, in between covering long distances on horseback, from all this can be gathered that John lived his teenage years to the fullest.

John promised the Uhlenbecks to write "in a week." Whether he did, we don't know. As far as we know, none of his eventual correspondence survived the onslaught of time. But, we do know that later in life John authored many columns for the *Glacier Reporter* and the *Hungry Horse News*. His columns attracted the attention of Senator Mike Mansfield, at the time representing the State of Montana in Washington DC.

Part II presents the outcome of Mansfield's interest in Tatsey's columns.

Part II

John Tatsey's columns in the 1957-58 and 1969 *Congressional Record*

Tatsey had been writing columns for some time for the *Glacier Reporter*. After Mel Ruder, owner of the *Hungry Horse News*, discovered this, he made a deal to also have Tatsey's dispatches published. In *Pictures, a Park, and a Pulitzer: Mel Ruder and the Hungry Horse News* (2000: 22) author Tom Lawrence mentions one example of Tatsey's "police-report" columns: "Joe Bird Rattler and Joseph Old Chief were doing some singing. Mrs. Bird Rattler told them to shut up but paid not attention so she called the police and poor Joe is serving out some time at the brick motel."

Senator Mike Mansfield, who represented the State of Montana in faraway Washington D.C. was a fan of John Tatsey's columns and would occasionally have parts of it entered into the *Congressional Record*. This drew an appreciative letter from President Truman, who said the column elicited a chuckle from him.

The *Congressional Record* is the official record of the proceedings and debates of the United States Congress, published by the United States Government Publishing Office. The *Congressional Record* consists of four sections, the *House* section, the *Senate* section, the *Extensions of Remarks* and since the 1940's the *Daily Digest*. Tatsey's columns appeared in the *Senate* sections issued in 1957/'58 and later in 1969/'69.[18]

Michael Joseph, better known as Mike Mansfield (1903-2001) had lost his mother at an early age and was sent to family in Great Falls. He served in the U.S. Navy during the Great War - yes, he lied about his age and therefore was later dismissed. He went on to become a professor of History and Political Science at the University of Montana. He was elected to the House of Representatives and during World War II he served on the House Committee on Foreign affairs. In 1952, Mansfield took a seat in the Senate and served as Senate Majority Whip from 1957 to 1961; during this time, he asked

---

18. Cf: mtmemory.org/cdm/ref/collection/p16013coll41/id/278 (last checked in July 2018).

his president permission to have Tatsey's columns included in the *Congressional Record*.

Mansfield addressed "Mr. President," then President Dwight Eisenhower, in the *Congressional Record* 1957/1958 as follows:

John & Belle Tatsey with Mike Mansfield.

STATEMENT OF SENATOR MIKE MANSFIELD (D. MONTANA)

John Tatsey—News Reporter.[1]

Mr. President, Washington, D.C. undoubtedly has the largest and most varied collection of newspaper reporters in the world. The Fourth Estate is represented in the Nation's Capitol by internationally known reporters and columnists, who are preoccupied with news and events of national and international importance. Many of these are known for their individual and distinctive style and technique. These news stories and features are read by millions in cities and towns large and small, but I doubt that any are read with as much avid interest as are the local news columns in the small weekly newspapers in this country. These news writers also have their own individual style and they are depended upon by their community residents as the source of news about their friends and neighbors. One of the most unique news reporters anywhere is the man who writes the Heart Butte news for the Glacier Reporter in Browning, Montana. John Tatsey, a Blackfoot Indian Service Policeman gathers interesting bits of news about his Indian friends in the community and prepares without a doubt the most unusual weekly news column of its kind. He makes light of incidents in these people's lives as do the syndicated columnists - who touch on the incidents in the lives of government officials and noted personages. As far as John Tatsey is concerned, his friends are of no less importance than any national celebrity. The weekly news column from Heart Butte on the Blackfoot Reservation may discuss the most recent inmates in the local jail to a man who motored to a Canadian Blackfeet settlement and returned with a bride. The Washington Post may have its George Dixon~ the Washington Evening Star may have its Fletcher Knebel,[2] but the Glacier Reporter and the Hungry Horse News has John Tatsey, Mr. President, I ask unanimous consent that few of John Tatsey's news columns reprinted in the Hungry Horse News, Columbia Falls, Montana, be printed at this point in the Congressional Record.[3]

Horn Downs Bottle a Minute

John Tatsey, Indian Service policeman, writes the Heat Butte news for the Glacier Reporter. Browning newspaper. Here is his column.

Sam Horn and his wife went to Browning last week. There Sam got orders from his wife not to cross the street from Yegen Hotel.[4] Somehow he managed to stop at the Legion Club to get a bottle opener for some pop so there he downed three bottles of beer in three minutes. Might be a record.

Father Mallman has returned from New York after spending his vacation there with his aged mother.[5]

Mr. and Mrs. John Tatsey motored to Deer Lodge last Sunday where they spent the afternoon with Abe Racine.

Thomas Many Guns was over to the Canadian Blackfeet early part of July and returned home with a bride.

Joe Running Crane is rather having a hard time by nog having a car. He left his car in Dupuyer to have it overhauled. He can not walk.

Stoles Head Carrier has quit his job at Valier and has been home. His wife left. She was afraid of drunks so she landed in Dupuyer where she would be safe.

Gerald Bauttier came home from Greenland where he was stationed. He will be home until September first and then go west to Spokane.

In, Out of Jail at Heat Butte

John Tatsey, Indian Service policeman write the Heat Butte news for the Glacier Reporter, Browning newspaper. Here is last week's column.

John Mittens has been hanging around town since his wife got in jail.[6] He is trying hard to get in there too.

Pete Day Rider has been home from the county jail in Conrad and had a party and his wife broke even on him by putting a gash on his head.[7]

Louie Red Head is serving a time in the country jail in Conrad. When they are in jail off the reservation they wish they were in James Walters place.[8]

Alvin Mountain Chief was picked up for not paying an old fine and a notice was sent to Indian police Tatsey for being AWOL and was taken by Air Force police from Great Falls last Monday. He got in a little trouble by running over a child with a car.

James H. Walters was around Heart Butte Sunday with his family.

The news the reporter gets from Heat Butte is true with a little joking mixed up with it.

Tom Williamson and Ted Spotted Eagle were in Havre last week where they attended a drivers school. They are going to transport school children from Swims Under and Mad Plume Schools.

Stoles is out this week.[9] Just wait.

Sunday was a very nice day at Heart Butte. Church was well attended and afternoon the boys had their regular stick game.

Mervin Brave Rock from Canada was here where his wife was confined to the hospital.[10]

Geo. Comes at Night pulled a stunt when he hid from his wife in town.[11] When she left he showed up at Jack Miles Pool Hall. Tatsey was sitting in car outside. Every ten or fifteen minutes he would go across the street.

Mr. and Mrs. Roy Doore were at the Tatsey place and had a picnic at Big Badger Canyon where John cooked some steak on campfire.[12] Maybe Joe Running Crane will try a trip like this.[13]

Some of the boys are getting back from haying jobs. One guy lost his wife. Some white guy took off with her.

Mrs. Richard Wild Gun has been missing for two weeks. She went to town to get some groceries. She was heard of at Starr

> School.[14] One boy has not been to work from Starr School since she has been there.

About twelve years later, Senator Mansfield again felt an urge to speak out about Tatsey's reporting. This time his good friend Lyndon Johnson was president. Perhaps something Johnson did, inspired Mansfield to again draw attention to Tatsey's columns.

On March 6, 1968, in an extension of his War on Poverty, President Johnson signed Executive Order 11399 to create the National Council on Indian Opportunity as an aid to the remaining 800,000 American Indians in the United States.[19] In a speech to Congress titled "The Forgotten American," Johnson stated that "The American Indian, once proud and free, is torn between white and tribal values; between the politics and language of the white man and his own historic culture. His problems, sharpened by years of defeat and exploitation, neglect and inadequate effort, will take years to overcome."[20]

Mike Mansfield and Lyndon Johnson.

---

19. How this Executive Order worked out can be read in Britten (2014). For further comments on this Executive Order, see: muse.jhu.edu/book/33397 (last consulted in June 2018).
20. For the full speech, see: www.presidency.ucsb.edu/ws/?pid=28709 (last consulted in June 2018).

CONGRESSIONAL RECORD - SENATE. TUESDAY FEBRUARY 18, 1969[15]

STATEMENT OF SENATOR MIKE MANSFIELD (D. MONTANA).
John Tatsey, News Reporter

Mr. President, it has been a long, cold, and damp winter here in Washington, and it has been a long, hard winter in many parts of the Nation. I think it is time for a little humor and the wry wit of one of Montana's best and favorite news columnists, John Tatsey, a modem-day Will Rogers and, perhaps, even better.

My old friend, John Tatsey, is getting up in years, but he continues to write sporadic news columns for several weekly newspapers in western Montana. As Senators may recall, he is a resident of the Blackfeet Indian Reservation and lives in the small community of Heart Butte. John's news columns are less frequent than in the past, but I have four which were taken from issues of the *Hungry Horse News* in the past year.

Mr. President, I ask unanimous consent to have these news columns, which appeared in the *Hungry Horse News* and the *Glacier Reporter*, printed at this point in the *RECORD*.

There being no objection, the articles were ordered to be printed in the *RECORD*, as follows:

From the *Hungry Horse News* and *Glacier* (Mont.) Reporter, Mar. 8, 1968]

JOHN TATSEY WRITES AGAIN
HEART BUTTE

(by John Tatsey, Glacier reporter).

Hello readers! It has been a long time since there was any news from Heart Butte, the reporter has been in another world for the past six weeks and found out that the people were missing his news.

Mel Ruder from Columbia Falls was around Heart Butte school taking pictures of the school and the students and the teachers.[16]

Mr. Ruder was at the Reporters home Monday to see if Tatsey was alive or sick, took pictures of the old log cabin.

A Mr. Tom from Cardston was at John Tatsey Place looking for Indian relics, he picked up a crow tail which is used by fancy dancers.

The Reporter was down around Wolf Point and Poplar visiting his daughter Mildred, she had the misfortune of breaking her ankle when she slipped on ice and fell but she is up and around with foot in a cast.

The Indian dance at Heart Butte was a good one, a lot of dancers and many visitors from Canada and Browning, everyone really enjoyed themselves, a lot of good coffee and eats, one or two staggered.

While in Poplar a Sioux indian was talking about guys drinking, he said one fellow was smoking a cigar and push the cigar to one side and stuck the bottle on the other side and drank and I told him what I saw in Browning one evening. I was in a room and a man came in about three sheets in the air and pulled out two bottles from both sleeves, opened them and stuck both bottles in his mouth and drank from the two at the same time. None ran out of his mouth. All he said was you win.

Old Stoles Head Carrier is really tied up, he has his grandchildren and cannot leave his son and daughter in law are in town, the daughter in law is in the hospital.

A letter was received from Robert James Grant who is at McNeil island and was wondering why there was no more news from Heart Butte.

The Reporter was in Cut Bank last week and ran into Jim Murphy an old friend and asked why I was not writing, he said the paper was not any good with no Heart Butte news.

While in Poplar went to a bingo game all indians. They sold lunches, berry soup, pemmican. All indian stuff and real good, all these were sold to raise money for this summers celebration, they said what has been collected is around $2200 and seven head of beef, this will be the last week in July. Good place to go and eat.

Latest on Stoles Head Carrier. On ground hog morning Stoles came out and saw his shadow and stayed home, someone came and gave him a carrot to chew on and someone else came along and gave him a banana and he ate that too.

Tim Morgan VISTA worker from Browning was out on Badger looking for the Reporter to get him to pick short stories of happenings at Heart Butte.[17]

(From the *Hungry Horse News* and *Glacier* (Mont.) Reporter, Mar. 17, 1968)

AT HEART BUTTE

[For the information of new readers, Tatsey columns have included such comments as follows:]

Pete Stabs By Mistake[18] and Mose Henault[19] were with the police Sunday at Browning. All they could bring was some grapes. They were so juicy they did not come home dry. Oliver Marceau was at police headquarters Thursday morning, and said he came home from Conrad, and forgot his wife there, but later she came home with her brother. Oliver was angry because his wife was sound asleep when they brought her.

Last Friday Louie Red Head went out in the field to help the hay crew. Supper time came and he did not show up and his wife was worried about him so she looked for him. She found him in Browning with the wrong women.

Last week Paul Running Crane[20] drove across the lopsided bridge on Big Badger when his car slid off. The front wheels hanging off. He jumped off, and left the women in the car, and now goes around long way.

Stoles Head Carrier was last seen in a pickup last week by Tatsey. He was laying full length and all that could be seen was his head and stomach. He was a little overloaded.

Tatsey was in Browning last week and saw Tom Lame Bear and Joe Tatsey[21] roaming the town. Tom Bear was last seen setting back of Teeple's Store and was sure crying as though someone died.

He was only lonesome for his wife who has been gone west some time ago.

Mrs. Lame Bear you are still remembered.

Mrs. George Wippert[22] of Heart Butte was telling of the earthquake what happened at her house. When it shook the children said maybe a horse was rubbing against the house. She felt a second one when her big Boxer dog was asleep under the bed when the dog started scratching under the bed.

[From the *Hungry Horse News* and *Glacier* (Mont.) Reporter, Mar. 22, 1968)

GOPHERS INDICATE SPRING ARRIVAL

HEART BUTTE.

There has been different animals showed up around that returned from the south. Kildeers and some gophers. Stoles Head Carrier showed up in Browning last week so it sure must be spring.

Joe Running Crane left last week for the hospital at Conrad where he is under treatment.

Aron Racine spent the winter at Heart Butte with his son Teke and last week his other son from Old Agency came and took him home.[23]

Lanie Red Head has come back to Heart Butte and stepped back into his old shoes.

There was a stick game at Wm. Running Crane home, a large crowd attended.[24] Badger Creek boys meet tuff opponents. Games lasted till 5:00A.M. Sunday, next day everyone was in sleepy hollow.

Andrew Round Man left last week on a short vacation and came home Monday with a head ache.

Henry Burd has been out on Badger Creek and is staying at the Joe Gallager home till he gets his own house on a foundation.

There isn't too much going on during all the good weather, everyone just laying around with spring fever.

Happening of thirty years ago, Chief Little Plume had a brother who was very near sighted, he goes all over. Little Plume told his brother don't go to the river because the slough is real high with waters and I saw a young woman standing in water up to the waist. So Stretch Out was the brothers name and he goes down toward the river and Little Plume saw him and got ahead of him and got in the water where the brother come in the water, Little Plume dove and pulled Stretch out under the water and he was calling for help. The brother pushed to shore and went home ahead of Stretch Out and when he came in Little Plume asked him where he had been and he told him what happened. He said what pulled him under the water was half woman and the other half fish. It was first topless dress. This is true. Next week there will be another story between these brothers.

[From the *Hungry Horse News* and *Glacier* (Mont.) Reporter, Mar. 29, 1968]

More about LITTLE PLUME, STRETCH OUT

(By John Tatsey, Glacier Reporter)

HEART BUTTE. - Second part of Little Plume and brother Stretch Out. He told him to stay away from the barn because there were some horses in there and they would kick him. Stretch Out went out of there house and was walking around and finally headed to the barn so Little Plume saw him and went ahead of him and stood inside the door, his brother came to the door with his cane saying whoa who, by that time Old Little Plume hit him on the chest and down he went and started to call for help. His brother pulled him up told him I told you not to go there or you would get a kick.

SELLS TRAP

The Reporter sold a Bear trap to Milo last week. He said he would set it in the door way and might trap a prowler. Better be careful Milo he might step into it when he comes home at late hour on a weekend.

The weather has been really nice and the people are sunning themselves.

There was a meeting at Heart Butte community building and a few attended. Object of the meeting was to plan a way to spend the money that is coming from the Sweet Grass claim.

There still having stick games on Badger Creek on Saturday and Sunday evenings. Last Saturday night there was a large crowd and some folks came all the way from Ronan, played two nights and went home winner.

BAD BOYS

There was a little trouble last Sunday evening when a young boy beated up on his grandfather. It is getting really bad when boys get that bad.

Mr. and Mrs. Joe Calf Boss Ribs and daughter Gene were at the Tatsey place transferring Indian songs from a tape recorder to a record player.

Joe Running Crane has been home after being in the hospital in Conrad and he is feeling fine.

The seventy to eighty year group are beginning to show up after the weather warm up but they are still under cover.

Stoles Head Carrier got some lease money and went to Great Falls to get a brace for his leg but ran into a friend and forgot it. He got some other klnd of bracer and came back to the reservation. Now baby sitting.

Tom Lame Bear has been gone for over a month. No one knew where went and finally heard of him being in Great Falls whose mooching is good.

One morning Joe was sitting in his house looking around and saw a Guy going house to house looking for opener.

In the column of March 17 Tatsey wrote: "Mrs. Lame Bear, you are still remembered." On March 29 Tom Lame Bear is missing for already one month? Did his mother die? What made him go missing? The Blackfoot digital library shows a photo of Tom Lame Bear John Mountain Chief with the subscription:

"John was a truant officer, which brought him great respect among the people. John was also the local all-around helper.

Anyone could call on him whether they were in need of help from the snow or needed a handyman. John was a very well-known and well respected man within the community."

Mansfield's interest in Tatsey's columns might have inspired Paul Devore to corral more of his columns. As we will see in Part III, so he did, while adding tales and teachings by the now veteran story teller John Tatsey.

Tom Lame Bear and John Mountain Chief.

Part II Endnotes

1. Source: *Mike Mansfield Papers*.
2. Fletcher Knebel (1911-1993) was a handful. He "advocated the legislation of marijuana, espoused the right to commit suicide - which he did in February 1993 and wrote three novels. From 1951 on he wrote a nationally published daily column, "Potomac Fever," and was called by President John F. Kennedy "Washington's most widely read and widely plagiarized" commentator (Lambert 1993).
3. Apparently Tatsey also contributed to the *Hungry Horse News*. This newspaper was started in 1946 and in 1978 sold by its then owner Mr. Mel Ruder (*New York Times*, November 23, 2000). In 2016 this newspaper celebrated its 70th birthday.
4. Sam Horn (*1905) was a son of Thomas Horn, but not mentioned at the DeMarce 1980: 130 page. Perhaps not yet born in 1907/1908? From now on, people that are not footnoted are not to be found in DeMarce or on other publications I am familiar with.
    Strachan Scriver (2006: 65) describes the Yegen Hotel, down-town Browning, as a "top-of-the-line place which leather upholstery in the dining room."
5. "A native of Germany, Egon E. Mallman, was ordained a Jesuit priest in 1929, in Woodstock MD. After a short stint as an assistant principal at Bellarmine College in Tacoma WA, he went on to spend more than forty years as a parish pastor on the Blackfeet Indian Reservation in MT. In 1977 Mallman moved to Mt. St. Michael's Ecumenical Center in Spokane WA and the following year to a Seattle parish, where he was in residence. He died in 1980. In 2011 Mallman's name is included on the Oregon Province's list of its members who have been identified as perpetrators of sexual abuse." Source: www.bishopaccountability.org/assign/Mallman_Egon_E_sj.htm (last consulted in June 2018).
    Prairie Mary (2007) writes that after 1935 Reverend Egon Mallman, S.J. "had to pick up the slack for the whole south half of the reservation when Holy Family closed in 1938."
6. John Mittens was born in 1896 and married to Lucy Fine Bull in 1916. Source: blackfeetgenealogy.com/pafg188.htm. Fuller (1898: 71) only mentions Jas. Mittens, son 3 years, Charles Mittens, son 2 years and Annie Mittens 5 years as children of Mittens 28 years and Susie Mittens 22 years.
7. Peter Day Rider might be the Peter, listed by DeMarce (1980: 84) as Peter, 8-year old, son of Peter Day Rider, 37-year old and Crawls Away, 43-year old, both full Piegan. From now on ages will be as indicated by DeMarce 1980. In Part I of this book, three years were added because Mrs. Uhlenbeck described people in 1911.
8. Tatsey refers to the jail in Browning as to the J.H. Walters Motel, the Walters Brick House, the Walters Hotel or Walters Den. See Tatsey in Devore (1971: 8), or in Part III of this book.
    There is also Abe Ernst Racine, who was married to Evelyn Spanish and later with Diane M. Chaffin (Blackfeet Tribal Business Council & DeMarce 1998: 263) and www.genealogie.org/famille/racine/mathurineng/aqwg64.htm#11450 (last consulted in June 2018).
9. Stoles or Stanislaus Head Carrier is not mentioned under the John Head Carrier (page 123) in DeMarce. Stoles is mentioned in (Tatsey's column cited in Doig 1978: 2003: "Something was wrong - Stoles Head Carrier has been staying home, he won't started to go wrong here … The Blackfeet seemed to be a rambunctious people."
10. Mervin Brave Rock, Blood, was the father of the Blood actor, Eugene Brave Rock (Volmer in *Calgary Herald*, *June 2017*).
11. George Comes at Night, might have been a son of Comes at Night, 55-year old and his second wife Double Charge but is not mentioned by Demarche (1980: 734). George or

Duffy Comes-at-Night was also a policeman. On April 15, 1962, while responding to a disturbance call, he "was ambushed at night, bound by his assailants, then dragged to death behind a horse. The 25-year-old officer was a Navy veteran and had only been a tribal police officer for a short time" (Hansen 2002).

12 Mr. and Mrs. Roy Doore were Roy H. Doore Sr. and Mildred Tatsey Doore, Mildred (*1923) being a daughter of John Tatsey. Doore was from the Blackfoot Reserve (now Siksika Nation), 90 kilometers east of Calgary. Also see, "This Cattleman: Roy Doore," by Frank Jacobs in Canadian Cattlemen 27 (10):5+ *(October 1964)*.

13 Joe or James Running Crane, a policeman, will have been a full-brother of Edward Running Crane, 37-year old, full Piegan (DeMarce 1980: 220). "John" who cooked something on fire will have been John Tatsey himself.

14 Mrs. Richard Wild Gun married Annie Mittens in 1910. Their son Richard was born in 1915. Source: www.blackfeetgenealogy.com/pafg203.htm (last consulted in June 2018).

15 Source: *Mike Mansfield Papers*.

16 In 1946 Navy veteran Mel Ruder founded the Hungry Horse News. In 2003 the history of this newspaper *Pictures, a Park, and a Pulitzer: Mel Ruder and the Hungry Horse News* was published by Tom Lawrence.

17 The organization Volunteers in Service to America was created by Lyndon B. Johnson in 1964 and blended in 1993 with the Corporation for National and Community Service, Americorps. Source: www.nationalservice.gov/about/who-we-are/our-history (last consulted in June 2018).

18 Pete Stabs by Mistake, 14-years old, was a son of Thomas Stabs by Mistake and Steal In The Daytime, both full Piegan (DeMarce 1980: 242).

19 Mose Henault was a son of Stephen Henault, white, and Caroline Henault, 1/8 Piegan (DeMarce 1980: 127).

20 Paul Running Crane, 13-years old in 1911, was a son of Edward Running Crane, full Piegan and Nellie Running Crane (DeMarce 1980: 220).

21 Joe or Joseph Tatsey was John's younger brother.

22 Mrs. George Wippert was Mary Weasel Head, full Piegan, 68 years-old, daughter of Buffalo Child and Otter Woman. George Wippert was her second husband, deceased. Weasel Head was her third husband. Mary Weasel Head died at the age of 90 in 1937. She lived across the tracks of the agency (DeMarce 1980: 270).

23 Aaron Racine, child of Oliver Racine and Belle Alverez, was married to Agnes Whitman and had three children, Donald "Indian," Calvin "Doekes," and Aloysius "Teke" (*Blackfeet Tribal Business Council* & De Marce 1998: 263).

24 William Running Crane, born in 1909, was a son of Edward Running Crane (34 years, full Piegan and Nellie Running Crane, $\frac{3}{4}$ Piegan, 29 years) (DeMarce 1980: 220).

Part III

The Black Moccasin

THE COVER PICTURE

John Tatsey

From an original oil painting
by Belva Curtis, well-known portrait artist.

PRINTED IN U.S.A.
C. W. HILL PRINTERS

The Black Moccasin

Compiled and Edited by Paul T. DeVore

Copyright 1971
LIBRARY OF CONGRESS
CATALOG CARD NUMBER 78-172559

THE CURTIS ART GALLERY
DAVENPORT HOTEL, SPOKANE, WASHINGTON

COLOR PHOTOGRAPHS

Back Cover — Winter scene on the Blackfeet Indian Reservation.

Page 7—John Tatsey and his 90-year-old Sioux wife Belle whose maternal grandfather was a brother of Sitting Bull.

Page 10—John Tatsey and his good friend Stoles Head Carrier. Stoles' fun-loving activities created colorful subject matter for John's newspaper column.

Page 15 — John Tatsey and his home on the Blackfeet Reservation.

Page 33 — Indian stick game in progress during Indian days celebration at Browning.

Page 36 — Belva Curtis, portrait artist, chats with Belle Tatsey in Hagerty restaurant in Browning.

Page 45—The skeleton of the last tribal medicine lodge on the Blackfeet Reservation.

Page 48—Peter Stabs by Mistake, grandson of Mountain Chief, last officially recognized chief of the Blackfeet Indians.

(All Color Photos by Wayne Curtis.)

ACKNOWLEDGEMENTS

To John Tatsey for giving us exclusive rights to reproduce his newspaper column.

To Mrs. Carl Minette of Cut Bank, Montana, for providing us with a complete transcript of Tatsey's column and newspaper publicity.

To Wayne Curtis for initiating the Tatsey book project and underwriting the costs involved in assembling manuscript material and pictures.

Preface

For seven of his 18 years as a tribal policeman on the Blackfeet Indian Reservation, John Tatsey (Weasel Necklace) wrote a weekly newspaper column for the Glacier Reporter at Browning, Montana. His long-time acquaintance with the Indians about whom he wrote, coupled with his keen understanding of their strengths and weaknesses, and a natural sense of humor, made his column a collector's item for readers and gained national recognition for its earthy portrayal of Indian life on the reservation.

To help capture the Tatsey humor and "bring to life" some of the situations and characterizations developed in his column, I asked Albert Racine, well-known Blackfeet Indian artist and sculptor, to prepare a number of pen line sketches. The captions under these drawings are taken verbatim from the Tatsey column.

And no report on John Tatsey would be complete without a word from his good friend Mike Mansfield, United States Senator and Senate Majority Leader, from Montana. On several occasions Senator Mansfield reproduced portions of the Tatsey column in the *Congressional Record*, calling the attention of his fellow Senators to the homespun writings of his Blackfeet Indian friend, as contrasted to the sophisticated reporting of internationally prominent newspaper correspondents in Washington, D. C. Senator Mansfield's introduction describes John Tatsey as an individual and as a portrayer of Indian life as seen through the eyes of a tribal policeman.

This book incorporates a reproduction of news items from the Tatsey column. No changes have been made in the Indian's wording, spelling or punctuation, or in his unique style of reporting on his daily contacts with fellow tribesmen.

The thinning in the ranks of the 19th century Indians marks the passing of one of the most colorful eras in the history of our original Americans.

Many of these Indians, born in the 1880's and 1890's, are unable or unwilling to talk about the transition to the white man's way of life. Few can recall the stories of

Indian life told them by their tepee-living forebears and few can relate the red man's version of events which played such important roles in their way of life.

John Tatsey is an exception to the rule. His remarkable memory and ability to communicate enables him to recount many of the colorful rituals of his people.

Learning of his story-telling abilities, I arranged a series of interviews to hear his interpretation of some Blackfeet names, legends and tribal ceremonies. This book, then, also includes a verbatim transcription of some tape recordings made in John's Heart Butte home on the Blackfeet Indian Reservation in Montana.

Editor

Introduction

It is often said that newspapers are as much a part of the daily diet of politicians as meat and potatoes. For those of us who are far away to serve Montana in the nation's capital, the saying is profoundly true. Papers like the *Hungry Horse News* and *Glacier Reporter* are the lifelines that keep us alive, and their contents nourish us with the spirit of home half a continent away.

That is why I especially treasure the writing of my old friend John Tatsey. His colorful accounts carry with them the true flavor of his time and place. The epic doings of Stoles Head Carrier and Tom Lame Bear assure me that, no matter what becomes of the Federal budget or all of the problems of war and peace, life goes on at Heart Butte with all its everyday pleasures and follies and complications—and above all, with the wry humor which the eyes of John Tatsey behold.

It is this quality of humor and the homespun—reflecting as it does a tradition and a way of life—which gives such special flavor to the events which are described by John Tatsey. His pen gives color and dimension to everyday happenings on the reservation that might pass uncelebrated by lesser scribes.

Not long ago on the floor of the United States Senate, I had occasion to refer to John Tatsey as a modern-day Will Rogers. So he is. For like Will Rogers, he reduces his observations to earthy commentaries that have a ring of truth for everyone. He pokes fun at life in general and makes us all chuckle a bit at our own absurdities. We are all better off for it. Because John Tatsey's view of life shines through everything he writes, it was inevitable that this book would be, in effect, both by and about him all at the same time. I commend it not only to everyone interested in Montana and its rich Indian heritage, but to everyone who enjoys contemplating humanity without pretense.

MIKE MANSFIELD
United States Senator and
Senate Majority Leader,
from Montana

John Tatsey

John Tatsey was born Jan. 26, 1894 near the site of his present home on the Blackfeet Indian Reservation. He is the son of the late Joseph Tatsey, a pioneer farmer and stockman, and Annie Langley Tatsey.

John's father, whom he describes as a "mixed up" Indian, was a Blood and his mother a Blackfeet. His mother had no Indian name but his father's name, Weasel Necklace, was passed on to John. He believes his grandfather, on his father's side, was an Englishman, probably a Hudson Bay trapper.

John's only education was at an Indian mission school. As a youth he did farm work and while in his early twenties operated a freighting business with horses. When machinery and trucks replaced the horse, he started ranching and got into the cattle business.

He was married in 1918 to Belle Alveraz Racine, a half-blood Sioux whose maternal grandfather was a brother of Sitting Bull. Her father was a Spaniard and served as a cook on boats plying the Missouri River between St. Louis and Ft. Benton. Now almost 90 years old, Belle was born near the mouth of the Milk River in northeastern Montana.

Two sons and a daughter were born to the Tatseys. Their older son was killed in the South Pacific during World War II. The Tatseys also raised seven of Belle's children by a former marriage.

In the early 1950's, Tatsey was named tribal policeman with headquarters at Heart Butte, a community of 200 to 300 Indian families, in the southern part of the reservation. He served 18 years. His ready wit and graphic description of his fellow tribesmen, especially those who imbibed too heavily of "gallo," led to an invitation to become a correspondent for the Glacier *Reporter*.

On several occasions during his newspaper career, Tatsey emphasized the fact that he was a truthful reporter. "I write the news that really takes place and happens," he said. "I won't make up any lies, just the truth. I'll back up anything I write."

6

His colorful by-lined column also evidences the fun-loving characteristic of the Blackfeet people.

"We tease the older ones and the younger they do the same," said Tatsey. "Like Stoles Head Carrier, he is a younger man than I am and I like to razz him. When I write about him I put a joke on the end. He would like to do the same to me, but he can't write. I got the best of him. I saw him in town the other day. When I see him I don't look at him. He bothers you, bothers you for money."

As a policeman, he saw the rugged side of everyday reservation life. Because he dealt almost daily with those who over-indulged in alcoholic beverages, the tribal jail at Browning became a "rest home" for many of his friends. In his column he refers to the Browning jail as the "J. H. Walters Motel," "Walters Brick House," "Walters Hotel," or "Walters Den."

The condensation of his weekly columns in the Glacier Reporter, which appears on the pages that follow, are not dated because weather, farm work or family affairs often interfered with the regularity of the reports to the paper.

Tatsey
The Newspaper Correspondent

NEWS ITEMS FROM THE INDIAN'S COLUMN
IN THE GLACIER REPORTER

with
Illustrations by Albert Racine

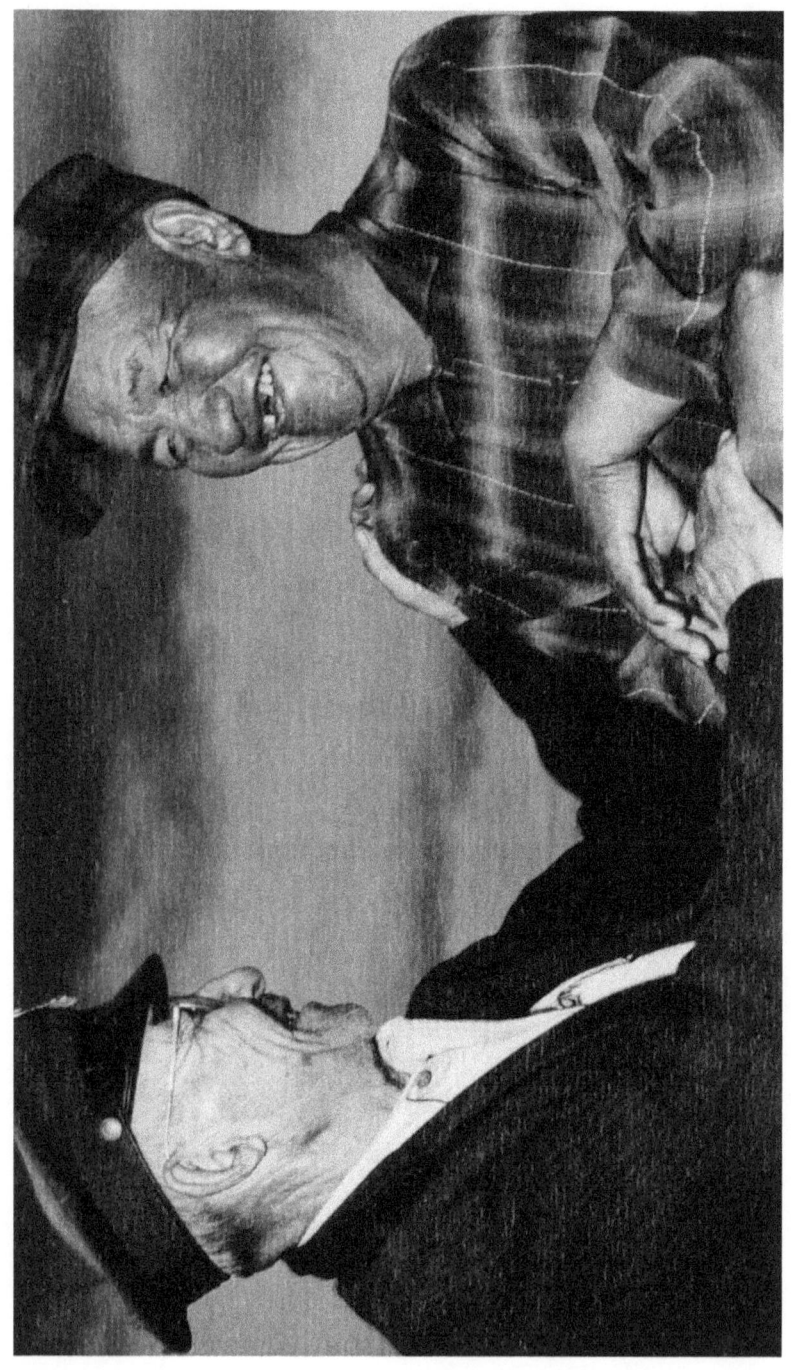

Heart Butte News

The best ever happened at Heart Butte was last Sunday when there were between 75 and 100 cars in front of the church. The church was jammed so there were a lot of people stood outside. Hope their prayers were heard.

Mr. Richard Little Dog has been coming to Heart Butte on Sundays. Tatsey had to put him in jail for the night. He came again last Sunday and someone reported so the police went to investigate, found him out in a car. Police asked his wife what was wrong. She said he was sick and his heart was stopping on him coming from Browning and stopped altogether when they got to Heart Butte. Police told them to leave and Richard's heart got back in motion. Too much gallo.

Francis Bull Shoe and partner Stoles Head Carrier are two fine men, staying home behaving.

Last week the Heart Butte twins were seen having trouble on the road with their legs. They were holding one another up to keep from falling. They got home sometime during the night.

Heart Butte people are expecting a lot of people for Easter Sunday if the weather permits. All will enjoy going to church and picnics and games in the afternoon.

The reporter from Heart Butte missed last week's news on account of the bad weather and blizzards, but will report what happened then this week.

On Tuesday the Council sent a load of Buffalo meat to Heart Butte and it was given out to the people and everyone had meat during the cold spell.

James Spotted Eagle was at police headquarters and reported dogs killing his sheep right in his shed at night. Police went to the party who owned the dogs and they were taken off the living list.

Leo Bull Shoe had a dream last week. He dreamed that he could take live coals from the fire and not burn himself so he tried it by putting live coals under his arm pits. Next day he had blisters under each arm so he is no medicine man.

Indian policeman John Tatsey had a little accident Sunday when he fell in a large bucket and could not get out. It took four men to pry him out. They almost had to get a torch cutter to remove him.

12

Leslie Grant went on a party with some young men last week. He did not want to go home, he was afraid of his wife so he went to Jerry Comes at Night's house and asked if he could sleep there till he felt better. They showed him a place to sleep where there was a person sleeping and it was his wife and it was all over.

Frank Comes at Night came to Heart Butte Sunday in a team and wagon and someone said the team and wagon blowed away with Mrs. Comes at Night in it.

Louie Red Head and son Lewis went out to look for their team of horses late one evening. Horses came home so Mary Red Head went out to look for her man. Louie landed in Dupuyer and found a team of Gallos. They ran away with him and Tribal police were called and finally caught him red hot, and kept him in the Heart Butte cooler and then over to J. W. Walter's quarters.

There is a new place at Heart Butte just south of the government square, where there are several people living. It has been raided a few times by Tatsey Tribal Police and now the name is Dizzy Land. There is competition between George Night and Maggie Jiggs for mayor in Dizzy Land.

Mr. & Mrs. Running Crane were not at Heart Butte Sunday and were soon missed by the people. They were stuck in a mud hole on Big Badger.

Sunday the Heart Butte children made their first communion. Fifteen boys and eight girls.

Mrs. Maxine Racine of Old Agency was hunting last week. She jumped a deer and pulled the trigger and shot her toe. Deer was safe.

Mose Henault started trapping at Heart Butte. Someone told him there were some beavers here that had skirts on.

14

Heart Butte News

People at Heart Butte all had a very good Christmas. All attended the midnight mass and Christmas day all had dinner with one another and evening they had feather games and stick game at the old tribal store.

The twins, Pete and George, are serving five days at the police woodpile, so they were out of mischief during Christmas.

Sam Horn of Heart Butte was a victim of the Tribal Police. He got in the rough court and was fined $20.00 by Tribal Judge Brown. Sam New Breast also was a short boarder at Jas. Walter's brick house. Lodging, $10.00 fine.

Joe Calf Bossribs No. 2 took Stoles Head Carrier to Valier Tuesday. Stoles bought some meat and liver and came home. Stoles took the liver and stuck it in the fire box and roasted it on live coals. Just when he thought the liver was done he told his kids that they better go to bed so they would not be late for school the next day. Next day they asked him if he saved any of the liver, and he said most of it burned in the stove.

Joe Day Rider said the Heart Butte twins went to Browning Sunday. They went in to buy with their relief orders. They were hungry for short ribs and pork chops. The older twin, George, rode the Blue Heaven wagon to J. W. Walter's quarters. He left $10.00 there for a tip to the city of Browning.

Last Friday Tatsey, the Tribal Police, went to Browning and drove out the Studebaker station wagon where it was in the shop getting some work done on transmission— little more speed for the summer.

James Spotted Bear from Browning was out Sunday to do some elk hunting. He got as far as George Wipper's place and spent all night cashing bones. He went home broke, he won't eat anything else but elk meat.

Something wrong — Stoles Head Carrier has been staying home, he won't go to town. He does wrong when in town and now has started to go wrong here. His aunt, Mrs. Caroline Day Rider, had him take care of her home while she went to town to get some things she forgot. When she got back Stoles was gone. She had a cake, cinnamon rolls and bologna to feed at a holy feather game. All were gone. Stoles had a belly ache for a week, he was at the stick game Sunday.

Mrs. Agnes Comes at Night was the only one caused some excitement when she walked over a little man sitting on the floor. She stumbled, fell against a candy show case, broke it and fell on the 140-lb man with 200-lb. weight. No one was hurt.

The police force have no mercy. Last weekend the Heart Butte trapper went to town in his trapping clothes, gum boots, and late Saturday evening was wading down the main stream in Browning looking for beaver signs. When the paddy wagon came by and took him for no trapper permit. Something was wrong — he did not know where he was till Monday morning before Judge Scriver.

On Monday a load of elk meat was brought to Heart Butte and the long sleepers were out early. Stoles Head Carrier was the head man in cutting and issuing the meat.

Police report on the Indian dance at Starr School was that it was one of the finest dances they have had in a long time. No disturbance by drinkers, it was just all good time.

Mose Hanault was gone for some time last week. Everyone worried about him because there was no one else to play rummy or crib, but he showed up Sunday in a silly condition.

Levi Aims Back was picked up Sunday night back of Geo. Wippert's place where he was hung up by one leg on a barbed wire fence. More fences would help the police.

Stoles Head Carrier was put up in city jail Sunday night. The boys inside were watching Stoles being searched and nothing much. He picked a pint from the overlap of his belly.

18

Heart Butte News

James W. Walters was over Sunday to go to church and pray for himself. He found out that he was away behind in his attending Sunday services.

Pete Day Rider gave a feather game, which is holy. A person will make a promise when they want good luck. Last October Pete was chased out of his house by his wife, so he promised he'd put on the holy. His wife took him back. Every time they get back together they put on some kind of a wedding party. It don't cost him anything to leave her.

Stoles Head Carrier came home from town and stayed with his family for Christmas. He came to the stick game Saturday night and sure enjoyed himself and he may be thinking of being a man during this year.

Sorry we did not have our news in last week. The reporter was busy butchering for the people's relief. There was five cows bought by the Tribal Council and cut up in small pieces. There didn't seem to be very many people, but last Friday there were over 200 names written down that got beef.

Old Big Eagle helped butcher two cows at Dave Hall's place and his son-in-law hauled him part way home. Then he loaded his two sacks on a boy's sled and took the power himself to pull it home. The boys took pictures of him, and he was layed up for two days. Maybe he ate too much, or too much pull.

Short article from Old Agency—Mr. Jas. Kittson hauled home one sheep, hauled it home in a one and a half ton truck, and one night the sheep got away. Next morning he tracked it going west. He lost the tracks up around Joe Arrow Top's field. Maybe they changed into human tracks. He got out of the sheep business in a hurry. It was no dogs to blame.

Louie Red Head, Sr., strayed away last week and could not locate him. He was wanted bad. The Indian police could not get him so Mrs. Red Head went to town and she got him. He is sure toeing the mark.

19

George Hall from Browning was out Wednesday after some boil meat. He sure likes soup with rice.

Calving and lambing is in full swing — and all going good.

Tatsey and H. Burd were patrolling Moccasin flat one day last week when they saw a man and woman by the grave yard fighting. She was beating on the man. He ran back a ways. When he came back to her he had a car tire around his neck. When she struck at him she hit the tire and bounced back. Dan Calf Robe was smart to think of getting the tire for protection.

John Aims Back got himself a deer last week. When he got home his horse got scared and John fell off and landed in 5 or 6 feet of water. But he still had the gut sack in his hand.

George Running Wolf, Sr., did wrong last week. He went after wood back of the church and came home without his axe. He went to look for it next day but never came back. He went through the pines and caught a ride to Browning and on into Cut Bank and there he came to, found himself broke, so he soaked his overshoes to get home. He is still in the dog house.

Wm. Running Crane had a little trip on his main road last week to town. He got in the wrong car and did not know he left his own car and family in town. Maybe there was a new one in the wrong car. They got him home. Next day he had a big boil on the back of his neck and his wife told him to be careful, next time they might break his neck. They squeeze rather hard some times.

Earl Shoots First and Hazel Yellow Owl were married at the church Sunday.

Tom Lame Bear was over at Hamilton for sometime and enjoyed his visit to his daughter. Everything inside never have to go outside, and come home last week and the high wind took his out house into the river. Bad luck.

From lower Birch Creek a young stockman had a bull that was lousy, so while it was a warm day he thought fix him up. He got the bull in the chute, and gave it a stove oil rub down. The oil went down to the skin and it being a warm day, he thought he had just as well brand it. He throwed a red hot iron on the bull and it caught on fire. Pretty sick. Bull hair all burned off.

21

Heart Butte News

Mr. and Mrs. New Robe went to Browning last week on business. They stopped at the Yegen Hotel. Mrs. New Robe went to the Tribal office while Vincent was left to baby sit. When Mrs. New Robe returned she found her 5-months old boy lying on the floor. Her man was really under the influence of liquor. She got just a little mad; she kicked him down the hallway. Then she called the police. He worked a couple of days and then got out of jail.

John Mittens from the After Buffalo community has not been around since his wife left home before the holidays. He sure must be lonesome. Women, have mercy.

The Heart Butte ground hog, Stoles Head Carrier, fooled the Heart Butte people. He did not see his shadow because he was in a dark place at the J. W. Walter's den.

Joe Running Crane has not been to police quarters for some time. Maybe he has a lot of coffee to drink or else there is too much snow, or his car won't go and he can't walk ten miles in the snow.

Tatsey, the Indian police, was coming up from Old Agency Monday afternoon and could hardly see the road. He was following a car track and came over a hill and saw a truck in the ditch, but too late. John was in the ditch, led by Father Mallman.

Mr. and Mrs. Pete Day Rider did a little sparring the other day, but Pete couldn't knock his wife out. He figured when she didn't get up he would leave, but she got up each time so he helped her in the house, and everything was loving as before.

Mrs. Dave Hall was taken ill last week and Dave took her to the Conrad hospital where she went under operation for appendix. She came home last week and she is all right.

Joe Running Crane and family took a short trip to Cardston, Canada, on business and also took in a dance there last Friday. They had a good time and also noticed two paddy wagons hauling passengers from the dance hall to town. Only forty-eight took the ride.

George Wippert, Chas. Weasel Head and John Aims Back were up to Dog Gone Lake hunting. They got one elk. Louie Red Head and John Tatsey rode horseback to the Heart Butte mountains and brought home a four-point buck.

The new school building at Heart Butte is coming right along. Wiring and plumbing all finished. It's sure going to be a very fine room. The best part is the gym has a fine stage. The men working on it are never idle.

Heart Butte ball team motored to Shelby for a game. They came back still full of pep even if they did lose the game. They are getting better each time.

Mrs. Geo. Wippert had a birthday last Sunday. Before the birthday party she was ailing with her back, and her sons and daughters pulled her around so much the next day she felt good—nothing ailing.

Richard Heavy Gun went to the Blood reservation Monday to visit a relative. When he got to the place a woman came out and he asked her where his relative was. The lady said "He is gone." "Where did he go?" "He died two months ago."

Stoles Head Carrier and some other boys were gathered for a song service a while back. Pretty soon a guy came in about half lit up. Stoles hit the door for home—left his overcoat and gloves. It was 20 below.

Hunters from the Heart Butte community have all returned with plenty of elk and deer meat, only they had a little rough time. It stormed all the time they were in the mountains, and coming out they lost some of their horses.

There are some women around with patched faces and some colored. That's because their husbands love them so much. That's the way Indian makes love. He beats heck out of his wife.

Louie Red Head went hunting along Black Tail. While going through a trail he met a black bear. He shot from his horse. The bear fell over and the horse sat down. Poor bear was about starved ready to die. Louie gave it an easy death.

24

Heart Butte News

Stoles Head Carrier was home while his son-in-law went hunting last week and came home at night. They told Stoles, your son-in-law is coming with meat. Stoles got out and helped unload and he cut a hunk of the solid meat and cooked it on top of the stove. He just browned both sides and went to the cupboard and started eating. When his grandchildren came to get a handout, he just pushed them away with the butcher knife he was using to cut the meat. And a little later the boiled meat was ready and he ate again. But he never got a wink of sleep the rest of the night.

Some boys from Browning were out to Heart Butte digging the grave for Mr. Chas. Iron Breast.

Joe Day Rider came up missing last week for four days and was about to be looked for when he showed up one morning early. He was a bit bloated from too much sleep.

Perry Spotted Eagle, the changeable man, something got into his mind and he went to church last Sunday. That was a good turn he made.

There is a young lady at Old Agency has started training in the feather weight division. She was spatting with her husband, she downed him and the next day he was wearing dark glasses.

Tatsey was in Cut Bank last week and visited the boys and girls at the county jail. They are doing well.

Last week the weather was so nice the people were so happy. Everyone was moving around in their shirt sleeves. But some of the boys went too far from home.

Tuesday Heart Butte school put on a party for the basketball team where they served a very nice lunch for the boys and parents and teachers. Mr. LaRue, teacher and coach, gave out the awards to the boys. Rev. Father Steinmetz from Valier made a very nice talk on sports and other games which the boys play. Heart Butte boys were sure interested. They heard some things they will keep in their minds.

George Comes At Night went to visit his little granddaughter on Two Medicine last week but landed in

Browning and the grandchild found him in Walter's quarters. Two night's lodging and meals cost him $24.00.

All the people that went from Heart Butte to the three celebrations came home sleepy and tired out, but all had a good time.

Peter Tatsey has got through cutting Aims Back hay meadows and has hauled 950 bales.

There were a lot of people at Heart Butte Sunday in spite of the bad weather. Some out of district candidates were around Heart Butte. People are going to have a lot of new friends and relatives from now till the June election.

Tatsey will have to investigate as Stoles Head has not been seen around. Maybe he fell off something besides a bridge.

There will be a lot of news this week when the people get their lease money. So readers of the REPORTER be sure and get next week's news. News will be gathered from all over the south side.

Jesse Black Man was picked up at a ranch last week disturbing a home. And when police found him he was in a hay stack, with just his head covered.

There were a lot of people in church Easter Sunday in spite of the cold air. Tatsey raided cars that came to Heart Butte with something to drink, so everything went fine after that. So boys, when you come, be sober.

Last Saturday there were two moose in Stoles field but when they left there they did not seem to fear at anything. They went up along the race track through Dizzy Land and when the people saw them everyone was after them on horseback, car and people on foot. It looked like Castro's army. The moose did not stand up long. Buster Yellow Kidney got one and Dave Running Wolf the other. The moose that were killed were tame ones owned by some stockmen. It was good meat.

Last Sunday Stoles Head Carrier was around enjoying the nice weather when some young boys saw him lying under a tree with a half a jug of wine. He was asleep and the boys took what was left in the jug and Stoles dog was with him. They caught the dog and poured the wine in the dog's mouth. The dog got drunk. The dog was still drunk Monday morning.

27

Heart Butte News

It's a good thing there are lots of pines and brush for cover at Heart Butte. Wm. Head got away from the police last Saturday night for disturbing peace in church.

Stoles Head Carrier was pretty well bruised up last week. When asked by police what happened he said he fell off a bridge.

The Agency road department were out on the Heart Butte road and did some scraping. Could be traveled with a little less bumps after.

Leo Bull Shoe did some bull-dogging last Sunday and Monday morning he was unable to get out of bed without someone helping him.

The new school building has some timber standing up and should be showing more later on.

Last Friday Louie Red Head went out in the field to help the hay crew. Supper time came he did not show up and his wife was worried about him so she looked for him. She found him in Browning with the wrong women.

Stoles Head Carrier has been to every reservation in Montana taking in the Indian doings. They feed a lot, so when winter sets in he will be in good shape.

The teaching staff at Heart Butte started Tuesday morning enrolling children. There are five teachers. The children should learn something.

Pete Stabs by Mistake and John Day Rider were out Labor Day and each got a deer while the rest were playing stick game.

It has been very quiet around Heart Butte since New Years. Maybe some new leaves were turned over.

Pete Stabs By Mistake and Mose Henault went with the police Sunday to Browning. All they could bring back was some grapes. They were juicy so they did not come home dry.

John Mittens lost his wife between Christmas and New Year's. He has asked the Heart Butte police to look for her but the police haven't located her yet. When they lose their wives they sure depend on their police. That way they sure get their wives back.

When the Medicine Lodge women camped, it started the big rain. So the stockmen and farmers should be thankful to Mrs. Swims Under. She fasted four days and the Lodge was put up on the first of the month. The following day there was a parade and dancing in the afternoon.

There were seventeen persons made the jail at Heart Butte during the celebration and now they are going to do some hard labor cleaning the camp grounds. All got 10 days. The law and order at Heart Butte are going to enforce their orders.

Billy Big Spring donated a beef to the camp and asked Tatsey to give the three persons who voted for him a good hunk of meat. There was a lot who voted for Bill.

Heart Butte people were all in sorrow when their leader, Philip Sure Chief, passed away last Friday. He was laid away Saturday. That was one of the biggest funerals at Heart Butte for a long time.

Leslie Grant and his son Merle went across Birch Creek on a haying job and Robt. Grant was going to work too. But the law got him before he got out of bed, and now he will work for J. W. Walters in Browning.

It was exciting when the tribal office caught fire. Don't know the cause of the fire. One or the other got too hot, that is the bills owed or too much new deposits.

There is a rumor around that Joe New Robe from Swims Under area has two porcupines staked at each door of his house so night prowlers won't bother. Can not depend on dogs.

30

Heart Butte News

Candidates for the Tribal Council for the coming year held a meeting here at the round hall to show themselves and their intentions if they get elected.

George Crawford was at Conrad where he underwent an operation for gall stones. He came back all right.

A new man appeared in the Heart Butte News Column. Tatsey was in town last week and was on the street when Mrs. Geo. Comes at Night came and told the police to tell her husband that she was going home and leave him. Minutes later Geo. came out and started to look for his wife. He had just enough drink to feel good enough and started on the run down main street. He beat his wife home. He was afoot and his wife in a car, so he should not have trouble in the coming election.

All drivers without drivers' licenses don't drive. The officer at Heart Butte has quit warning you. You will be picked up and turned over to the state patrol.

There are two boys working at Heart Butte serving a ten day jail sentence. Tatsey used the old way of sentence the old full-blood judges used to do. Saw wood with a saw that has no setting and clean and scrub the jail so it will be nice and fresh for the coming lease payment.

Emmett Brewer is doing some spring cleaning at his place—snow, old hay and manure have collected.

Swims Under school and Mad Plume school had their school picnic together and was well attended, about 250 parents and children. Plenty to eat and lots of ice cream for the children. Races were run and prizes given. A baseball game was played between Gamblers and Winos, game won by Winos. Harvey Monroe was in the fat women's race and was beat bad, and played ball and was just getting limbered up when it was over.

Francis Bull Shoe has done all right since last week when he landed himself a Civil Service job, so he will be off the bad news column.

One of the Heart Butte twins strayed off to Browning and some candidates gave him some stuff to drink and when he landed himself a Civil Service job, so he will be off the bad news column.

One of the Heart Butte twins strayed off to Browning and some candidates gave him some stuff to drink and the city police drug him out of a mud puddle and put him in Jas. Walter's care. That's the older twin.

There are some children, boys and girls, that would like a place to stay and work for the summer. Anyone interested may contact Bill McMullen or Police Tatsey.

John J. Tatsey has filed for broken down seat in the tribal office from the Heart Butte district. Everybody knows John is a friend of everyone. Have good reason to try for a councilman. Already cost thirty cents.

During the last two weeks there not any news from Heart Butte on account of the weather. The reporter's pen froze up but will write some when ever it warms up where people start moving around.

Found between Old Agency and Heart Butte, one license plate and tab, truck 38-T1210, Tab No. 38T1204 and one lady's shoe with overshoe. Owner don't be afraid to call for these because the jug was empty that was there.

Heart Butte has been in peace since the boys are at the jail.

The Indian dance at Heart Butte was well attended. People from all over the reservation and some from Canada. All had a good time and plenty to eat which consisted of fried bread, boiled meat and coffee. The dance ended at two-thirty.

One day last week Joe New Robe hitch up his team and told his wife to go with me and cut some poles. When they got to where they were to cut when Joe saw a black animal come out in the open. Joe said it was a black cow. Joe tied his team to a tree and got their poles and the dogs took off through the brush and the dogs came yelping it was a black bear. Joe grabbed the gun but could not load it. She was in the wagon. Joe handed her the gun, she loaded it and she told him jump in and we will go. Joe did, took the lines and started whipping his team but they would not go. They were still tied to the tree. Bear just stood there laughing.

Some boys went fishing Saturday at some beaver dams. Phillip Dog Gun was getting strike in the meantime the ice was going down when he noticed it and he slid down in the water above the waist. Every time he tried to get on the ice it would break and he would go down again. No one has taken a bath like this this time of year.

34

Heart Butte News

The weather has been warm and so nice that the people are moving around, and taking care of their loved ones' graves.

Stoles Head Carrier came back from Canada with not much mischief, only later news came to this reporter that the Canadian Blackfeet gave him a name which fits rather tight — Chubby Stoles.

Joe Running Crane was a camp Police at the celebration. He spent most of his time as gate man. He leaned against the rail for three days. The rail was green when put on and dried out when Joe was leaning on it — it stayed bent.

The Indian Summer is sure making people roam around and not thinking of the coming winter they get out early and stand around in there shirt sleeves, but I guess we can enjoy things as they come.

Stoles Head Carrier has not been seen since he came out of the mountains. He was in Browning and in Conrad, getting different brands to get the soreness out of his body, none helped. Only a bigger head ache.

Last week some folks woke up and saw it snowing. Looked around to see where they can get some wood to cook their breakfast. Wasted Indian Summer days.

There has been a tooth puller at Heart Butte the past week taking care of bad, bad teeth. Remember Heart Butte people, there is some elk meat coming this winter and might be tough.

John Tatsey was called on the phone last Monday to be in Browning at 11 a.m. When Tatsey arrived in town he went to the High School where coffee and rolls were served. When Senator Mansfield came Mr. & Mrs. Tatsey had a picture taken with him. Mike had his medicine pipe with him but did not offer Tatsey a peace smoke, so Tatsey did not take him into the tribe or give him his Indian name, but still we meet and made friends.

Boy John Aims Back has not come home from potato picking. Instead he is peeling potatoes in the county jail.

35

Mose Hanault the trapper was at the church last Sunday. He was trapping on Big Badger and someone came along and stole his traps. He is sure mad. Return traps or keep out of his way.

James Black Weasel of Durham had some trouble of someone breaking in his house and took all his groceries and now he hides his bacon and sugar under his pillow. So Mr. Indian Thief, be sure to look under pillow.

Some of the people went to Conrad to do some shopping, and they all managed to come back through Dupuyer. From there they came home fighting and singing.

Joe Running Crane has been pretty lucky all the time he drove a car. But since the car quit running he fell down and cracked his wrist.

Since our trapper Mose left Heart Butte there are two new trappers came in and started to trap. They are from the old Agency way. Their first set were real good. When they went to look over the trap line George Edwards went one way and Dexter Galbraith went the other. George brought back two magpies and Dexter brought George Kipps' pet dog and one skunk. The beaver still to be caught.

Tatsey has gone back on duty the first of the month and will enforce the law. There has been too much mischief went on while he was vacationing.

Mr. & Mrs. Roy Doore and family were at the Tatsey place, also Peter Tatsey and family. All enjoyed dinner but there was one who did not enjoy eating a tough chicken. Dick Doore—he forgot his false teeth in town.

Stoles Head Carrier left last week and has been missing since. He was in Dupuyer. He came home Monday, he drove his car in with no tires. He won't move into camp. He has a look out stationed among the jack pines by his house and that's where he will be watching for the police car.

Joe Running Crane gave Joe Arrow Top a ride out to Old Agency with some groceries. When he got off at his house his wife and kids took off for the brush. They were afraid of him. In the meantime dogs ate up his meat and other stuff. Next morning his wife asked him if he had any money left. He told her he saved three $10 bills. He said the dogs ate those too. He kept two dogs in the house waiting for them to vomit. Dogs held tight.

38

Heart Butte News

Dogs has been killing the Bull Shoe sheep and Francis killed five dogs. So dog owners watch your pets. The Heart Butte police will help in destroying these killers, so don't get mad.

Henry Evans was caught in the rain—no dry wood in the house, so he took one of his overshoes to cook breakfast and the other for supper. He won't need the overshoes this summer.

An Indian got mixed up with an old lady at Heart Butte so the old woman pick up a jug of Gallo and whack him over the head and his head was soaked in wine. He was hospitalized for several days. So don't bother an old lady.

On the 25th of May there was a roping and bronco riding at Francis Bull Shoe's place and were some good ropers and riders. George Comes at Night came out kicking his horse after a calf. When he threw his rope hit the calf on the rump. The horse stopped quick, George fell forward and on down to the ground. He was top heavy.

We have had a sickness among the middle-aged people which hits the vicinity once in a while over night. The Indian doctors called it Gallio myelitis. It kills some for about 12 hours.

Joe Running Crane went hunting Sunday and got a deer and he sure got soaked in the rain waiting for it to get dark so no one would see that he had meat.

James H. Walters turned over two boys to Tatsey at Heart Butte for education, in the line of work. Aloyious Weasel Head and Eugene Head Carrier sure know how to wash dishes now. At Heart Butte they are being taught how to chop wood.

There are now six teachers at the school. The new teacher came last week from Missoula, Mr. Richard Gregory teaching eighth grade. The first day in his school room he really froze out. His stove was not working right.

There was some excitement last Wednesday when some folks come and reported there was fighting at Caroline's Joy House. When police got there everyone was quiet, but Guy was covered with blood. So Tatsey took him to town and he got stitched up some.

Richard Heavy Gun and family are in Canada for the Medicine Lodge celebration which will last a week. Stoles Head Carrier is in Canada where he is going to join in on the Sun dance. Stoles would get set to start blowing the whistle, and rain would start and would delay the doing.

There was the Wolf Point Herald drifted in the Blackfeet reservation. There were statements in it where the Sioux and Assiniboines are fighting over their tribal council men and some of our democrats in D. C. We would not want to see our good Friend Mike Mansfield scalped. Better get a short hair cut.

Mose Gilham and his son Robert who came up from Georgia last week and were walking down the main street of Browning when they met a big fat guy. Mose said that was Stoles, the one you read so much about. Mose said that Stoles never bums money. When they got the introduction Stoles said, give me 50 cents.

Perry Spotted Eagle, Vincent New Robe, Fredie Old Rock were picked up by Tatsey on warrants for not paying their fines when they promised to get out and get the fine money. Boys, better settle with James H. Walters—you may need a room some time.

The State Superintendent of Schools was here for the day at Heart Butte. There she was inducted in the tribe and given the name Morning Star Woman. The name was given to her by Sam New Breast, Sr.

Johnnie Calf Face told his wife he was going to the store and get some thing but never returned. The store keeper said he got some gas and said he had to get to the hospital as he had an infection in his arm. Maybe it was an infection in his stomach.

Mr. & Mrs. James H. Walters motored to Hot Springs where Jim bathed on Sunday afternoon and got home O.K.

Paul Running Crane was driving along Badger in a rubber wagon. His dogs kept barking at the horses. Paul got mad and whipped up and started chasing the dogs with the team. He hit a rut or badger hole and fell out. The team kept on going.

The dog catcher was around the Moccasin Flat looking for dogs when he came upon a little boy playing with three dogs. The man asked the boy if his dogs had licenses, and the boy looked up at him and said my dogs don't need licenses because they don't drive. They walk and run.

41

Heart Butte News

Bernie Wilson and Tony Sarno from Browning were at Heart Butte last Saturday evening with a man from Seattle checking up on some boys. The wind was blowing so hard that the gentleman lost his hat, so old Napi has a hat for the summer.

Harold Douglas, game warden, was at the Tatsey place Tuesday just pestering around.

Paul Running Crane was fooling around some horses in a corral when he got too close to one and the horse let Paul have it on the right cheek with a left hind foot. May need X-ray.

Police Tatsey chased the wrong drunk last week. This was off the hiway where the police car lost one rod. Drunk had good medicine.

It sure has been nice weather the last few days and many people were able to come to church. James Walters was out from town to attend services. He has more faith in the Heart Butte church.

A sheep herder went wild for several hours Monday. He had two guns, shotgun and rifle. He stuck the shotgun in the belly of his boss. The boss got away and came straight to the police quarters at Heart Butte. The Pondera county officer came late in the afternoon and drove out to the camp and got the man out in the open country. Tatsey was going to use Indian style on him—run circle around his sheep wagon.

Mr. Wolstad from lower Badger reported to the Police that there were a pack of dogs that got into his sheep over the Jackson coulee. Lost quite a few. He said he would like to save a few to ship.

Last Sunday Tatsey drove down along the White Tail creek and saw some one go around a hay stack to hide. When the Police drove around, Stoles was out in the open and James Comes at Night was standing against the stack sound asleep. Don't know when he woke up.

Mrs. Francis Bull Shoe and daughter Mrs. Eagle Feathers came back from Flandreau where she had a visit with her son. Nice trip. Patty and Peter Tatsey Junior were along. Patty said she saw Crow Indians at Hardin. She said they were short and fat.

The School Program was one of the best for a long time. The children did really fine and one boy by the name of Hot Dog had the crowd laughing all the time.

Mose the trapper was hired by Richard Heavy Runner to trap some beaver. He made his set and caught two that night. He told Richard he would take some wine for pay. If he did not get that he would turn the beaver loose.

Stoles did some trapping. He caught one large beaver. He brought it to town and asked big money for it but wound up getting $1.50.

John Tatsey has his log cabin in pretty good shape for the winter. John is going after elk this coming week and we'll have dried meat and back fat.

All tribal police have the two way radios in their cars and are really handy. So boys, be more careful.

At the last law and order meeting it was suggested to arrange to send off some of the bad wino cases to Warm Springs. It might help a lot.

The old time doctors who first came to work among the Indians claimed that they could cure drunkenness by injecting horse blood in their veins. Maybe now it would be better to inject horse sense into their brains. Might help some.

Mr. & Mrs. Louie Red Head motored to Sun River Monday to engage a job.

Lost—Dan Calf Boss Ribbs was to put on a medicine pipe smoke. He went up to the store to buy some tobacco and landed in jail. Never came back for a week. He made his medicine at Walters' Hotel.

Heart Butte reporter was given some yearling heifers and were branding when one heifer backed up and kicked the reporter on the ribs and cracked one rib. Wore a corset for a week.

Sunday morning there was a little rumpus along Big Badger. Pop bottles flying and popping the guy. Sure beat it. Women don't hold back when they want to hit their husbands.

44

Heart Butte News

Some of our people at Heart Butte went to Conrad to put on an Indian show which turned out real good. They enjoyed the buffalo barbecue. Everyone was filled up so they really put on a dance in the evening.

Mose the trapper was two short on his traps when he picked them up. Beavers did not get away with them. He thinks some two legged beavers got them.

The reporter got crippled up Tuesday by trying to help a cow get up. She throwed her head back and hit the knee and he can just walk to get by.

Stoles Head Carrier got in the big money last week. The first thing he did was to buy a Nash car. The last he was seen was on the Two Medicine on the short cut to Heart Butte sitting with two flat tires and no gas, and has his car brought in for repairs.

George Tatsey from lower Blacktail was in Browning. Got some boys from James Walters place. He has them bucking bales of alfalfa. They will sweat the Gallo out.

Police Tatsey and Stoles Head Carrier met in Great Falls last week after they were dismissed from the court house and took in the town. Tatsey saw Stoles down on skid way with some girls from Hill 57. He managed to get one in the car and told his son Gene that he has new mama. Then he went to sleep and his girl friend got out. When Stoles woke up he was home, still in the pick up truck. No girl, too bad.

Richard Heavy Gun and Stoles Head Carrier have been working around Fish Lake last week and came home for the week end but they stopped in Dizzy Land for an hour. When they left there they were all so dizzie they did not see Tatsey parked at the gate. They were put in the Heart Butte sober up tank till next day, and on to J. H. Walters.

Last Sunday night there were a couple women got drunk and sure gave the Police a bad time. But Joe Running Crane piled them up and sat on them till they were locked up, but Joe was out of wind.

Mike Mansfield was through Browning last week and wanted to know if his friend John Tatsey was in town. Tatsey was disappointed in not meeting him.

Last week Henry Crawford found one of his sheep shot through the neck, but did not die yet. Hunters, there is a big difference in game and sheep and cows.

Mose the trapper came to Heart Butte but moved back down to Badger to start trapping. He says he cannot work late because his head lights are failing.

Last week Tatsey and John Aims Back came out of the mountains and got the meat of deer out O.K. but really paid for it. Lost 3 hunting dogs by getting poison along the trail by some dumb trapper.

Heart Butte may have a Mexican rally as one of our candidates has some Mexican blood, and he may make a good one. Blackfeet mixture might work out all right.

Report from the Starr School way some boys were rounding up some cattle they were going to ship and were chasing them with a Jeep when they got too close and broke one cow's leg.

Reporter has not been around Heart Butte to pick up the late happening but will get everything in the next week news so readers don't be disappointed.

Mrs. John Eagle Ribs took her nephew Stoles Head Carrier to an Indian doctor in Wolf Point. This Indian bleeds his patients till all bad blood comes from out his veins.

All potato pickers have all came back from the Cascade area. All managed to get home with a sack or two of spuds.

Stoles is still on the unable list, but was in town and sneaked in a few nips of Gallo.

Stoles Head Carrier came home one evening he was all wet. They asked him what happened. He said he was helping some beavers building a dam. They found some of his clothes by the dam.

Tuesday afternoon the reporter was driving to Heart Butte and saw two guys on the road. They seemed to be arguing over something when they got to the store it was Geo. Bremner and Robert Still Smoking. Robt. said that the Cree was sure dumb. He put up a sign upside down and Geo. said that the Blackfeet could not read. Geo. had to stand on his head in order to see if the sign was put up right. Both blamed it on their nationality.

49

Heart Butte News

Our good friend Stoles Head Carrier had a stroke last week and has been at the hospital for some time and improving. If he don't get well he will die.

Sunday was a busy day visiting candidates at church and at the rodeo which was held at Francis Bull Shoe ranch. They were a lot of people where riders and ropers were loosing up for the coming big rodeo at Browning. Joe Wild Gun and Francis Bull Shoe were unlucky—when Francis threw his rope his horse stopped quick and Francis kept going. Joe went next. He caught his calf when he jumped off.

There was a prowler at the school yard Saturday night, knocking at doors. When Tatsey went out to investigate he found Joe Middle Rider from lower Two Medicine. Lucky Tatsey was on a vacation, with no jail keys, so stay away Joe.

George Montgomery was at Heart Butte Monday. Took the trouble of coming just to take a movie of Jerry Comes at Night on a wagon and family showing how the Indians used to move around. So we will see Jerry on movie this winter—maybe TV.

John Aims Back has been sitting in the dark after the storm last week. After hunting Monday in the mountains he got snow blind.

Mr. & Mrs. Francis Bull Shoe motored to Great Falls Saturday. Returned in the evening. Francis has started lambing.

Joseph New Rope was invited to Browning for the Indian Days. He was pretty gaunt when he got home. He said when they passed around the eats all he would get was bubble gum. He was just learning how to blow bubbles when the camp broke up.

Last Friday evening there was a bingo and lunches sold, and the proceeds went to the church at Heart Butte. There were a lot of people there showed good faith toward their church.

Gilbert Spahn of Badger rode up to the foot hills just

riding around when rode on to two elk. Got both so Francis Bull Shoe will be eating elk meat till spring.

There has not been much going on at Heart Butte, only candidates from both partys roaming round giving treats and smokes.

John Running Crane predicts the coming winter. He said geese are high and muskrats in close to shore and Old Napi got a good crop of berries. So let's wait and see what happens. He says open winter sounds good.

There were a few guys that took sneakers from there wives. Some of the women offered a reward for there men, but 7 cents was not enough, and some were glad to get rid of them.

Young folks are out at night chasing and killing jack rabbits which are worth little money, so the only thing ain't bothered is the porcupine. John would pay 50 cents for a few for making head dress.

Our tribal council members have sent a delegation to Mexico for some thing the tribe isn't sure about. Some say that they went there to see if they could get some Mexican fish to plant on the Blackfeet reservation.

The Blackfeet Tribe Basketball team were at Heart Butte where they tangled with H. B. Warriors. Score 26 to 50 in Tribe's favor. The girl twirlers put on a show at half time. All had an eagle feather in there heads. Juanita Williams, Linda Hirst, Patricia Tatsey, Phyllis Sure Chief did a fine showing.

Francis Bull Shoe was riding up along Badger Creek looking for horses. The younger boys don't like to straddle a horse all day, only it takes Francis a little time in getting on and off.

Some of the dancers from Heart Butte were at Starr School stepping off the different Indian dances. There were lots of visitors from other tribes. All enjoyed a real good time and many gifts were given. The dance was a real Indian celebration. Plenty dancers all in beautiful costumes. It was lively till 3 a.m.

The reporter got a Xmas present from the Glacier Reporter and left it in town. A nice fruit cake. Did not get to eat it on Xmas day but had pinto beans and jack rabbit in place. Can't go hungry.

Saturday night some boys were riding in a car Geo. Aims Back bought and when the police was after him. When they drove into a bull pine and the car straddled the tree. That was the end of the run. Next day one of the boys had a patch across his nose.

52

Heart Butte News

Louie Red Head was over on Little Badger at the Bull Plume place with their recording machine making records all Indian songs.

Jerry Looking Glass had trouble with his eyes and could not see good enough to play stick game and was sent to Great Falls to eye doctor. When he came back he had on dark glasses and boy, he's hard to beat.

There was a meeting called at Starr School Sunday to explain the aims of the Blackfeet improvement association to the people by John Harper, Vic Connolly and John Tatsey. Harper explained in English and Tatsey in Indian. The plainer it was told, the worse the people thought of it.

Stoles Head Carrier was at the horse races Sunday. After a while he came out of an old creek bed feeling mighty fine. Good thing he had good teeth. He could not use his hand so he opened his bottle with his teeth.

There was a piece in the REPORTER sometime ago where it was mentioned they are going to give a big prize for the best teepe at the next summer Indian days. That may ruin the teepe outfit. One will get the $500 and the rest won't get anything. Treat everybody equal.

Sunday was rather bum on account of the boys being all gone. Mostly old folks and women left — all cars around Heart Butte were all being driven by women. The men were all gone fighting fires.

Some of the fire fighters came home and some left for the fires that are still blazing. Around the barracks building was really crowded with women waiting for the fire bus to meet their husbands. Wonder which one they will be glad to see — their man or the check.

Chief Big Eagle did not feel very good and was mad at the same time when he heard some company was coming on the reservation to locate a place for atomic waste. The Chief heard that they were going to blow up Four Horn lake as the storage site. The only place to catch the fat fish.

There was a white guy came from down east when he heard they were taking Indians to fight fire so he goes and signs up. They asked him his name and he said his name was Daniel Running Bear. It will be bad when the white man gets to using the Indians' names.

There was a meeting held last week on the irrigation problem. And another thing they are fighting is trying to lease the southern part of the reservation for atomic waste. This is only part of the reservation has more full bloods and still is Indian owned land, and they don't want anything like that put in by the white man. They are crowded in this corner. They don't want to be pushed out to some hill 57.

A new community has started up at Heart Butte in the last two weeks which used to be known as the side hill, and now it will be known as Dodge City because the people that live there have been dodging from house to house and finally to the river. Big partys put on by the boys. Getting rough.

Henry Evans has been having a tough time. Beavers are daming the spring so he can not drive his car to the house. One dam below the crossing, the other above. He tears one down while they repair the other. Henry, give up.

Some one went to the tribal office and saw Joe the janitor hitting with a fly swatter from one office to another. He was sure sweating, but had to make some showing for the day.

Joe Running Crane is going to try and make a drum before Christmas. He'll have enough deer skins. His brother-in-law got 4 deer last week.

Mr. & Mrs. John Little Dog were at Heart Butte Friday evening attending a little song service held at Jas. Little Dog home. Everyone enjoyed singing and the lunch served. The balance of the night was spent at Geo. Wippert place playing stick game.

54

Buster Yellow Kidney was out on Big Badger after the storm to try out his deer hound he got. When he got out there he jumped some deer so him and the dog started on the run. Buster looked back. His dog could not keep up with him.

John Tatsey had to put a new born calf in his kitchen to thaw it out. It took all day Monday to get on his feet and got belly full Tuesday.

Heart Butte News

The reporter last Friday morning drove out to check on the sheep he supposed to herd. While looking around saw a white tail buck. Wanted liver so bad for breakfast. couldn't shoot to hit. No guts there.

There were George Horn from Durham at Heart Butte with a Canadian and his wife. They were at the stick game all feeling really light. The Canadian asked someone where the rest room was, and he was told there was none, but to do the best he could to find one.

The wedding dance at Little Badger turned out pretty rough. Towards morning a free for all, but the bride and groom got home without a mark.

John Tatsey has an invitation from Governor to attend inaugural for 16th of January. First Republican ever invited a Democrat, but the tribe has no traveling money.

As I say, I write the news that really takes place and happens. I won't make up any lies, just the truth. I'll back up anything I write.

Our long time stockman Gordon DuBray passed away last week. All felt sorry for him.

The reporter has been doing cowboy work for the last three days rounding up cattle. Painful to walk now.

The reporter from Heart Butte lost all his blankets out at the self service laundry last week. Some one came and asked if the blankets were ready and he got them. When the reporter went after them, the other John had already taken them. The manager said someone just looked like me. Hope for return.

Reporter took his pickup to Valier for an overhall job. He has been driving a sorrel horse instead of a buskskin Ford.

The reporter and Louie Red Head will see their names on the bill board next week. Let's have another full blood Indian name for the council. Louie Red Head is a full blood and very smart, with a lot of experience in life and the condition of the full blood tribe. Very kind and good hearted to both old and young.

Thanksgiving day was rather poor for a dinner at some Indian homes, but were thankful for what they had. The full blood Indian shared what he had with Mother Earth by taking some of the food and putting it in the ground. That's how thankful they were.

Joe Running Crane took his oldest son to Shelby last week to shop. He told Joe he want a long sheepskin overcoat. He found one cost him $65.00 and no money left for groceries. He'll keep warm till the next check comes in.

Felix Running Crane has been busy plowing road in Mad Plume community from one house to another and the short piece to the main road. He is the only one that has a team of horses.

Sam New Breast received an invitation to the President's inaugural which will be Jan. 20 in Washington. Have to get along without Sam. No money.

John Tatsey, the reporter, Carson Boyd, Peter Red Horn, Earl Old Person were at the Montana Mansfield dinner which was at Helena last Saturday. There were a lot of people there around 7 or 800. There were ten tables and all full. There was not any fancy stuff on the tables but the roast meat was real good because it was black angus beef. That's what Mike Mansfield enjoyed. All Montana officials were there. There were a lot of good words for Mike. The reporter from Heart Butte talked to him, and he said to the Reporter, it's been a long time since we ate together. The reporter said yes, and Mike said yes and it's been a long time since we got any news from Heart Butte.

This is Mountain Chief who, according to John Tatsey, was the last recognized chief of the Blackfeet tribe. Mountain Chief, a Piegan, represented his tribe at the historic recording of the Indian sign language in 1930.—DeVore photo (See page 67.)

58

Tatsey
The Story Teller

AN INDIAN VERSION OF TRIBAL NAMES,
LEGENDS AND RITUALS

From Tape Recordings Made
in John Tatsey's Home on Blackfeet
Reservation

59

How the Blackfeet Tribe got its Name

"WHILE THEY WERE all together and before there was any division in the country they didn't have any name right then but were called savages. Later on after they grouped up they got to calling them by their chief. There was one head chief above all and he had four subchiefs under him. These five, the chief and subchiefs, had their own bands. He was the leader of so many people and usually they were called after what they did, mostly. The head chief was over the whole band together. And none of them had any name, that is the band.

"The head chief he had 10 wives . . . you think that's enough? . . . He had 10. They were all sisters or related. The first wife was the older and they were all related. He married her and later on he got the next one to her and on down to the youngest to the relationship among the women.

"Well, he had two or three tepees as head chief; one was his and the other two were for his other wives. The one he lived with was the youngest one. They had their own tepee. Just the two of them. The older women they worked for the old man, sewed his clothes and made his moccasins and cooked for him. The youngest wife didn't like that. She was jealous. She wanted him all to herself.

"Whenever these women sewed moccasins for him they would take them over to the chief's tepee. His young wife would accept them but when they left she would put the moccasins in the fire and burn them up. The old man had one pair of moccasins. Believe his first wife had made them. They were black and greasy, just like a stove. But his young wife wouldn't give him any new ones.

"When the rest of the tribe would have their meetings then he would go there without putting on any clean clothes, that is buckskin suit or moccasins. Toward spring of the year he called a meeting saying 'now we are going to go different directions to hunt.' This time would be about in June, what we'd think now, when the service berries would be good and ripe and black at a certain place. And when that time came they would all be there, the whole tribe.

"They would have a sun dance and other celebrations. When they got ready to move, each chief took his band one direction, just like that. All scattered out to find the buffalo.

"So when that time come, or before, after about a month, it was quite a little while, there was a young man from the head chief's camp there who went and told the chief 'I'm going to go and visit a certain tribe.' They had a way of knowing which was which, you see. 'I'm going over and visit my relatives.' That was all right. So he went. But when he got to the camp the chief there heard he was from the head chief's camp, so he invited him to his tepee for something, a meal, something to eat and to smoke.

"He went into the tepee, so they greeted one another and sat down. So the subchief asked him, 'How's that blackfeet chief up there?' That's where the 'blackfeet' first come up. The blackfeet chief. The young man knew what he meant and said, 'he's all right . . . the same as ever.' Of course they were talking, talking, visiting. Then they went on. So that summer after they had their celebration and after they had grouped up toward fall and got to mentioning where they would winter. When that time come the whole tribe was there. Must have been any way, as we figure now days, that is counting you know all the Indians that told it said there must have been 2,000 or 2,500 in this one Blackfeet camp.

"So when they got back to their winter camp, they had a battle with the Assiniboins. A whole mob of them. They fought there for a half day, I guess. Towards sundown well the Assiniboins got licked, whipped. Even if I have a Sioux woman, we had them whipped.

"These warriors, they started to come back to camp with whatever they took from enemy, with all their scalps, guns, arrows and everything they had got in the fight. They all came back, but they missed their chief, the Blackfeet chief. They were just getting ready to go out and look for him, to look for his remains, I guess. They were just about ready to go when they seen a rider come

61

111

The Blackfeet Indian Nation, as this road sign on the east side of the Reservation explains, is composed of the Piegans, Bloods and Blackfeet proper.—Curtis photo (See pages 63 and 64.)

Indians have been tanning hides for generations. Primitive methods have undergone many innovations as illustrated by this picture.—Curtis photo (See page 64.)

up over a little rise. He was singing. I never learned the song, he was singing a victory song.

"He had blankets and he had guns, arrows, spears and scalps. And then, I think, he had six horses with him. They were all loaded with these different things, what he had took from the enemy. There was a big circle of tepees and right in the middle there was nothing. He rode into this and hollered and everybody came into the center of the camp. Everybody went. He got off his horse and stood there with the other chiefs and they sat down in the circle.

"He told them, after they got through smoking, 'now we had the fight this afternoon and this is what I got. You see those horses and everything that is on them. When I give you all that, today, right now, I will accept the name "Blackfeet." The man that called me that . . . that is a good name and I'll take it and today we are the Blackfeet Indians.'

"And that name has been going ever since. The Blackfeet tribe. So that is how it has come among the Blackfeet. That fellow had dirty, greasy moccasins because the young wife wouldn't fit him with new moccasins. The older ones did it, but she burned them up. The buckskin suit he had was one of the best but she wouldn't even let him put it on to go to these gatherings, just the way he was, dirty clothes and slouchy, and people noticed that. So that is how this man noticed it and called him the 'Blackfeet' chief."

How the Bloods and Piegans got Their Names

"They gave each of the bands a name. The Bloods they gave them the name because when they find game they eat the insides, like the liver, kidneys and that stuff and their mouths would be all bloody. They still carried our name with them. The same as the Piegans.

"That Piegan name is, how that comes in, is that in Indian we call it Pikuni, either way. The meaning of that, there was some women in one band they were fast workers, done everything fast, in a hurry. They would tan these hides into white buckskin for their tepees. When they got them all sewed together and the tepees set up and when the sun hit it hot, you would see spots where the tanning didn't go through. They did too fast a job.

"So from that, they, the white man, called them Piegans, or in Indian, Pikuni. The white man would say albino. Piegan means albino. So that bunch got that name.

"And then it goes on. Some one band camped out on the prairie, and they called them Buffalo Chip Burners. These chips dried till they burned just like wood.

"Then it goes on to other bands. They called one band the Black Door band. So when they have their tepees they got a black robe or something for their doors against a white tepee. They called them the Black Door band.

"Oh, there's a lot of this. The Black Door and Buffalo Chip Burners belong to the Blackfeet, just smaller bands and they travel around with each of their chiefs.

"About giving them names. That still goes on here. When I moved in here and built up here, this band right here, 20 or 25 families, they lived here. Another band they lived up the creek four or five miles. That is another group and there is another group down here. That group in right here they called them Lone Eaters. Whatever

64

The Badger creek valley where more than 200 Blackfeet Indian families make their homes. The valley settlement is known as Heart Butte.

they get they eat alone. When you cross the bridge up here on this creek, that's the Black Door group. Another group on up the creek, they call them the Green Burners. In the winter time they burn green wood and it makes a lot of smoke. Their head man, they call him White Man. That was his first nickname. His dad was a white man. He was light, had blue eyes and wore beads.

"Another camp they called that the Lone Coffee Makers because this head man he would get up early and put a pot on the stove and make coffee and he would drink it all by himself. He wouldn't invite anyone to drink any with him. So they called them the Lone Coffee Makers."

The Last Blackfeet Chief

"M<small>OUNTAIN</small> C<small>HIEF</small> was a Blackfeet. There were three Mountain Chiefs. The last one died here about, at least 12 years ago, maybe longer. That was the last chief we had. His dad was Mountain Chief and his dad (grandfather) was Mountain Chief. This was the head chief of the tribe. It came on down, as the old one died, it came down to this last Mountain Chief.

"Now a day, everybody is a chief. I am a chief. The white man they call anyone on the reservation a chief. I never been able to figure that out.

"How they came to be called Mountain Chief. This was told to me by Mountain Chief's grandson, Peter Stabs by Mistake. He told the story.

"Years ago there were 12 or 14 men, we don't know whether they were soldiers or what they were, but they were in uniform, some kind of uniform. They were along these mountains looking for the Blackfeet camp. So they went along and along and got away up there to the Chief Mountain.. They went to the top of it and looked down in the lower country, open country. While they were there they spotted this big camp, out in the open. They saw it was a big camp with many horses. They rode down there and rode up to the camp. They asked where the chief's camp was. They directed them there and they went over there. The chief came out and asked them into the tepee. They got off their horses and went in and sat down. Of course the old fellow had to fill that pipe, you see, a long-stemmed pipe he smoked with these men.

"Anyway, after they got through smoking, I suppose they ate something. Then they got ready to go, so this head man of the white men, when he stepped out he called the chief and told him to come out too. He must have had an intepreter or something. He told the chief 'I'm going to show you something. I am going to give you a name.' So the old fellow said 'I'll accept that.' 'Now you see that mountain up there. That stands out away from the rest of the mountains and it's high. And you are down here with a big camp and you are the head chief

67

above all these people. I'm going to call you "Mountain Chief." I'll give you that name. And we will call that mountain "Chief" Mountain.'

"So that's where the Mountain Chief and Chief mountain came from. I kind of figure it might go back to the time of Lewis and Clark. They were in this country about that time. It was the grandson of the last Mountain Chief that told the story."

The Indian Sign Language

"WE GOT OUR OWN SIGNS to talk between the Blackfeet. I learned about sign language from this old man I used to work with who was hard of hearing. He made signs and from that I learned it and I understood what he was saying. These Blackfeet signs they could be understood by anyone. Of course, some of the old timers would meet another tribe. Of course, the signs would be a little bit different but still they managed to make each other understood.

"I have had that experience with Gros Ventre, Sioux and Assiniboins. Some of them don't talk English and I can't talk Sioux. I had to make signs to them. There's very few signs they make that are like ours, but still I'd made the signs and could catch what they were talking about. Could ask them to repeat what it was they meant by the sign. They managed to understand.

"The same way with the Bloods, their signs are the same as ours. We talk the same language. The Sioux, Gros Ventres and Cheyennes, their signs are just a bit different, but not very much. The sign for horses is a common sign, also cow horns and buffalo hump. It's plain.

"The only sign language I never could understand was the white man's sign language. This old John Clarke, he'd use our sign language and then he'd mix it up with the white man's signs. I'd tell him, Ya, I understand. (The late John Clarke, a deaf mute, was a well-known Indian sculptor.)

68

"Then there was the smoke signals. That takes a little explanation. Let's talk about the hills first. One person will be there and start this fire. The smoke goes up and you take a blanket and fan it. And the smoke goes up. That's the sign for smoke signals. There a lot of things a person don't use but still we know what they are. They got three or four signals and when they hit that smoke, a ball of smoke will go up and will go up quite a ways before the next one. They count these whoever they are making signals to. And whatever it is, three or four, those people over there know if it is their own kind or somebody else. The signals won't be the same.

"I don't know where they ever got a looking glass but they used to use that. They had little ones they used on the sun to signal with to show what direction they should go to get away from the enemy if they were in sight some place.

"There was a lot of times they used scouts, they generally have two. They never let one go alone. They would always have two. They were far apart, maybe a quarter to a half mile apart. They go to the highest peaks and get up there and will look around. Whenever they spot an enemy, he comes back or else makes a signal to the main band. They come on up and he explains just where the enemy is. Then they start to sneak around and get ahead of them, the direction they are coming, and just when they get so close, then they charge."

Editor's note: In the words of the late General Hugh L. Scott, Indian fighter and peacemaker who directed the government recording of the Indian sign language at Browning in September, 1930, "the sign language, based on ideographic gestures by the hands, grew out of a need for understanding between Indian tribes . . . it is the imitation of acts, qualities and attributes . . . it is a description of a thing by color, shape or what it does . . . it is the lowest grade of language but obeys all the laws of linguistic science, save those of sound . . . it appeals to the brain like any other language, by the same arguments of vocal speech, the only difference being that it appeals through the eye instead of the ear."

These Indians, all in full tribal regalia, represented the 14 plains tribes called to Browning, Montana, in September, 1930, to officially record the Indian sign language. In army uniform at the right is the late General Hugh L. Scott, former chief of the general staff of the U. S. Army and official interpreter of the sign stories told by the Indians.—DeVore photo (See page 69.)

70

The Blackfeet were Good Warriors

"Blackfeet were good kind people and were mean when disturbed. They fought for their hunting grounds and their land. They never looked for trouble, they just went on their war parties and whenever they were attacked, they fought . . . they fought to win and wouldn't stop for nothing. All tribes admitted the only Indians they were afraid of were the Blackfeet. They run the Assiniboins and Sioux to where they belonged. The Crows were trying to come up this way and the Blackfeet kept them back. And the Nez Perce, they tried to get in here. Well, they run them back.

"So that's why they claim this whole territory between here and the Yellowstone River and down around the Little Big Horn. Some of this is our territory, too, but they stayed there and that is how they happened to be there at the time of the Custer massacre. And that is Blackfeet territory.

"The Crows admit that there was an Indian from here, he stood 6½ or 7 feet tall, a big Indian. The Crows used to call him the 'big nigger.' He was a dark Indian, real dark. He traveled alone. He would go along these mountains clear down there. When he got straight west of the Crow camp he would get down there. He would take what horses he could from them, but some say they knew it was him and they didn't bother him. They knew he was alone but they were afraid of him . . . they never followed him. His name was White Quiver. He was the greatest horse thief of the Blackfeet."

The Medicine Lodge

"The Sun Dance and the Medicine Lodge are both the same deal. They got the two combined. It is the same thing. The Medicine Lodge, that has got to be performed by a person or persons, men and women, that are good people, with no bad intentions of any kind, live a good, decent, straight life. They're the ones that puts that on. And how they get that, some other people that have had sickness in their family, or someone gone somewheres, well, they take what we would say a vow that this person gets well or returns safe. And if that happens, everything comes out all right.

"And when the time comes for their sun dance, the Indians all get together in one big camp and one tepee is set up in the center for the medicine men and women. There would be five or six that are in this medicine tepee praying and singing.

"And when they perform this Medicine Lodge or Sun Dance, they have these people that have been sick or have returned from the service or war; they have them in there and paint them, paint their faces, and pray, thanking the Lord or the Sun that they returned all right. And they have other things they do. Like they cut the tongue out of a cow, or from a buffalo in the old days. They cut that and dry it and boil it and give it out to the people, just a small piece, as far as they can make it go around.

"When that's done, they then go to the center of the Medicine Lodge and put up that center pole, with a lot of dry roots and different things. After putting up the center pole, the men that do the whistling, face the tree, and the other people in the back praying. And when that is over with then they put the trees and leaves covering the Medicine Lodge; they put them at the entrance to this place, and they build a fire there. And the Old Timers they get in there and review their war days, their fighting. They fire guns and dance around and they show how they scalped their enemies, to make a success of their Sun Dance.

"This goes on for about four days, and when that is

done, then they have their dance, they perform that, and when that's all done, then the regular celebration starts, the people having their good time for the rest of the week, where they celebrate for about 10 days.

"But now they don't do these things any more. It is just simply dancing now. No more Sun Dance.

"Where the Sun Dance started. It was given to the Indians through the Thunder Man. That's what the Indians called him, I think it was. One young man was taken to the Thunder Lodge where there was an old couple living. And this couple had a boy, and the Indian boy found this other place. I suppose it was somewhere there he found this boy, and took him home, wherever he lived. And that's where the legend of the Sun Dance came from. It was given to this young man from these people that lived in the Sun. This was called the Thunder Lodge. They showed him how the Lodge was built and used, the poles that went to the center pole, down to the ground to make a circle, it was right to the ground to the top of the trees, the center pole.

"In later years, after the Indians practiced it regular, they had posts on the outside circle, and they had posts on top, plumb around. I'd call them rafters on the outside, plumb around to the middle of the center pole. That's the only change the Indians made themselves."

Origin of Family Names

"MANY OF THESE NAMES come from war feats. But now we still use what a person does, or is in a habit of doing something.

"Like myself, I have an English name and an Indian name both. My English name is Tatsey but my Indian name, among the Indians, is Weasel Necklace. My people they either captured or killed an enemy with a weasel necklace, so that way my dad got that name from that deal and when he passed away well I got the name. My son has his own name, but I can pass it on to my grandchildren if I want to. There is nothing legal about this. But it is in Indian ceremony that name is passed on. Some of these cost a lot of money. (Tatsey has given his Indian name "Weasel Necklace" to his long-time friend Wayne Curtis.)

"The older people they don't call me by my Indian name, some of them do but most of them don't. The only way they know who they are talking about is that they say 'that fellow that's got Sioux woman for a wife.' That way they know who I am. I'm the only one with Sioux wife, I guess, around here.

Stoles Head Carrier

"That there, the name Head Carrier, his dad's name was Head Carrier. His dad got the name from an old man. I saw the old man, he used to live down below Old Agency. Let's see, what was his name? I can't think of his name. But anyway, it was either his uncle or his dad, he got Head Carrier for a name. His name was John Head Carrier, that was Stole's dad. I call him Stoles for short, his real name is Stanislaus.

"But the nickname the younger people called him was Black Bottle. He got that name, we called him Black Bottle in Indian because he got a birthmark right here on his stomach. I saw it. I finally saw it when I was a policeman. I was dragging him out of a house one day. Well, I pulled his shirt up, you know, and when I was ready to load him, well, his shirt was way up and his pants was halfway down. I seen this birthmark, the bottom of the bottle was here and the open part was here. And its shape was just like a bottle with a neck on it. So that's how he got the name Black Bottle in Indian.

"But Head Carrier, that comes in way back. The old timers that were still fighting and his dad or grandpa or somebody when they came home from the battle, he was carrying an enemy head, so his people they called him Head Carrier. See, he was carrying this head, so that's where the Head Carrier name comes in. That's a war name, too.

Peter Stabs by Mistake

"He's a grandson of Mountain Chief. He knows everything. If he could just talk. He is a full blood. Didn't go to school much. About as old as I am. He knows the stories so good. He tells me these things and that is how I learn. I write them down. That is his English name. His Indian name is Red Boy. That's his original name. When his mother looked out and saw this red cloud in the west, she told the old man 'we will call our son Red Boy.' So he got his name from the red cloud in the west.

Swims Under

"That's another war name. There was another group that was on a war party. It was winter and the enemy found that they were around. Then when they all took off, one got left. He got behind. The rest got away. And the enemy was coming. The only chance he had was to get under where there was an opening in the creek. It was ice and he got under there. He got under the ice in the water. So he was swimming all the time to get away from the enemy. Swimming under the ice.

Comes At Night

"That fellow, that's away back, too. Whenever he went any place he never did come into camp, his own camp, in the day time. He always came back with what he got at night. If he got any horses or any scalps, he always got home at night. So that's why they called him Comes At Night.

Chief All Over

"There was this other group or band of Indians. They called them Chiefs All Over. That's a band. This band,

75

they all wanted to be chief of their band, you see. So another band of Indians would hear about that and they called them Chief All Over. So that's where that comes in.

New Robe

"That's something about a robe that was taken out of an enemy camp or off a horse, an enemy horse. A brand new robe and whoever took it from the enemy horse or camp, when he got to his own camp, he presented it to one of his friends and the one that took it called one of his sons New Robe. It was an enemy's new robe, a brand new robe. When this was given to one of the Piegans he called his son New Robe. We have one New Robe left and he's up there lying in the hospital.

Singing All The Time

"When she was a girl that was all she ever done, I guess. Playing and singing all the time. So they just called her that because she was all the time singing, happy all the time. She was my grandmother. She was a full blood Indian. Been dead maybe 60 years. (Tatsey has given this name to Belva Curtis.)

A Blackfeet Battle

"THERE WAS A BUNCH, they were mostly Blood Indians from over there in Canada, they went down on the Red Water, south of Wolf Point. I think there was 13 or 14 of them and they had these two scouts going. Of course, the other party they had their scouts too. But these Bloods, they don't see the scout at all. They see the main band down there. So this enemy scout he runs out to his bunch and they come on and they charge these Bloods before this other guy could get to his own party, you see. When he did get there it was too late. Well, they surrounded them and wiped them out.

"This other one (Blood scout) was on the other hill and when he saw what happened, he just took off. He figures there was no show for them to survive. So he took off, and he was the one that told the story when he got back.

"A Sioux Indian down there, he died a few years ago, he told it. He said he was in that battle. He was a young man when they fought.

"He said there was one man that was brave. They had a dugout or a wash out and that this was where they got in and that was where they were shooting out of to shoot the Sioux out there. This one Blood Indian got down in the deep washout and he followed it quite a way from where they were fighting. When he was going through the washout, there was a bunch of big sages, sage brush. And it was hanging over the bank and he got under that and hid himself under that. He just set there and he could hear them shooting and yelling and singing everywhere out there.

"Well, one man from the people that was fighting, he walked along a way out from the rest of the Indians and he was coming up this washout and he was walking along. And he was looking down in the washout and when he got to the sage hanging over he seen this man sitting there. They both saw each other, their eyes met. This man that was walking he had a black blanket and he had his hair down, cut off. It was a sign of mourning. He had two sons

77

that were in a battle with another tribe some place else and they were both killed.

"He seen this man sitting there and he went on. He was thinking. That's what this Sioux Indian was telling me. He was thinking 'now, that poor man sitting under that bank with sage brush over him, my two sons must have felt the same way, couldn't get away and couldn't save themselves and they got killed. Maybe they tried to save themselves, tried to get away from where they were at and I suppose this poor man here he wants to live and get back to his people.'

"That was the thought he had in his mind. So he goes right on and never mentions him at all, you see. So this man in the hole just set there and he could still hear one or two up there still yelling, still living and fighting.

"Just before dark, when everything was quiet, he pretty soon could hear the horses loping over the ground, their feet. Just when he didn't hear any more, he gets up and took out in the direction he come in from the rest of his people. This other one (Blood Scout) was ahead of him, they were behind one another, but they never got together. They were the two that told the story. They were both on the Blood Reserve.

"That's quite a story. That Sioux and Blood Indians, they tell it the same way. Just how it happened. That's why they call it Red Water. It is just a little dry creek. Right there where they done this fighting there is all kinds of Indian stuff, like beads and flints. I would like to get down there sometime and look it over."

The Editor

Paul T. DeVore, who compiled and edited this book, is a former Montana newspaperman.

A graduate in journalism from the University of Montana, DeVore served on the editorial staffs of the Helena Independent and Great Falls Tribune, and as associate editor of the Montana Farmer-Stockman. Since 1940 he has been engaged in agricultural journalism work in St. Paul and Spokane.

The Black Moccasin Endnotes

Page 6
- For a discussion of Black's 1960 dissertation *The History of the Holy Family Mission Montana, from 1890 to 1835*, see Prairie Mary (blog of April 13, 2007).
- Belle's grandfather, Spotted Elk (1826-1890), was a brother of Sitting Bull. Belle's parents are listed as Morning Star (*1823) and Plenty Horses (1854).
- Belle married to Oliver Racine in 1899 and had seven or eight children with him. Source: www.genealogie.org/famille/racine/mathurineng/aqwg36.htm and www.accessgenealogy.com/native/oliver-racine.htm (last consulted in 2018). Later she married John Tatsey and had several children with him.
- Thomson & Johnson (1976: 126,127) state that the E.J. Gallo Winery started in a rented Moesto warehouse in 1933 and "grew into a colossus with more than 175 million gallons of fermenting and storage capacity with annual sale exceeding approximately 100 million gallons of wine, in the Tatsey columns called 'gallo." The Gallo philosophy was "Make wines with flavors that appeal to huge numbers of people, and do it reliably."
- Heart Butte: in 2016 the population was 582: suburbanstats.org/population/montana/how-many-people-live-in-heart-butte (last accessed in June 2018).

Page 11
- Richard Little Dog (*1904) was a son of Mike Spotted Bear from Siksika, Canada. He was married to Louise Spotted Bear. Their children are Louise, Forrest, George, Donald, Hazel and Lorraine Little Dog (Hungry Wolf 2006: 1149) and www.archives.com/1940-census/richard-little-dog-mt-16989199 (last accessed in June 2018). More about Little Dog and his Sacred Pipe Bundle in Strachan (2008: 284, 285).
- Francis Bull Shoe (1887-1974), recorded six hours of Blackfeet Indian stories in 1973, which are for sale on a 2007 CD as *Blackfeet Oral History*.
- James Spotted Eagle, 35-year old, ¾ Piegan, was married to Mary Spotted Eagle, 25 years, full Piegan (DeMarce 1980: 240, 241).
- Leo Bull Shoe might not have been a medicine man but in 1976 was a Blackfeet elder and can be seen measuring and cutting a drumhead from cow hide on: aifg.arizona.edu/film/blackfeet-14 (last checked in July 2018).

Page 13
- Frank Jerry Comes at Night (1909-2002) was married to Lena LaFromboise († 1972). Frank Comes at Night: he worked for Forestry, for the Green Thumb program and was a truant officer at Heart Butte School. He was the oldest elder in Heart Butte, member of the White Shirt Society, original Heart Butte Society member and member of the Crazy Dog Society. He enjoyed playing stick game, loved to sing and play banjo, guitar and harmonica, enjoyed horse races and pow-wows, spending time with his children and grandchildren and playing blackjack." Source: www.cutbankpioneerpress.com/news/article_830e4a0a-eecb-5ac9-8299-a525f4be3875.html (last consulted in 2018).
- George Night Gun, 7 years old, was likely a son of Wallace and Mary Night Gun (DeMarce 1980: 191).

- Maggie Jiggs was eh, well, could Tatsey have made here a reference to the Maggie and Jiggs in the *Bringing Up Father* cartoon series?

Page 14
- Maxine Racine was born in 1922, married to Aloysius Racine. According to the 1940 census, he had one son, Gary: www.ancestry.com/1940-census/usa/Montana/Aloysius-Racine_2q9f3b (last consulted in June 2018).

Page 16
- On June 19, 1911 Mrs. Uhlenbeck described George Day Rider as: "When the Henaults left also, George Day Rider came in. What a beautiful Indian! What handsome figure. He is young, about 23. What a beautiful complexion. His black hair hangs neatly over his forehead. And the shape and expression of the face is so beautiful, and so soft & friendly."
- Peter Day Rider, 8 years old, was a son of Peter Day Rider (son of Frank Mountain Chief) and Crawls Away (DeMarce 1980: 84).
- Sam Horn, 4 years old, was a son of Thomas Horn, full Piegan, 35 years old and Many Different Gun Woman, 34 years and ¾ Piegan (DeMarce 1980: 131).
- Sam New Breast was married to Agnes, a sister of Joe Iron Pipe. According to Mrs. Betty Cooper (2013), her brother-in-law Sam New Breast, his wife and young daughter died when the Swift Dam collapsed, "sending a wall of water down tiny Birch Creek." Source: sixtyfourflood.com/2013/08/01/passing-into-history-3/ (last consulted in July 2018).
- On August 2, 1911 Mrs. Uhlenbeck wrote in her diary: "Time and again I look around for our interpreter. Tatsey stays away, but there are visitors: John Red Fox, Joe Day Rider, a big 17-year-old boy" [...]. On August 19, 1911 she noted: "George was busy, he was going around with two bottles of whisky - a prohibited privilege! - bought outside the reservation & had been fighting with Gobertz, a half-breed, camped near the Gardepies." In 1921 George Day Rider farmed six acres of wheat with Albert Mad Plume (Hungry Wolf 2006 IV: 1160).
- James Spotted Bear was born in 1909 and later on married to Agnes Spotted Bear (*1914). Source: www.ancestry.com/1940-census/usa/Montana/James-Spotted-Bear_2nmr4q (last consulted in June 2018).

Page 17
- Mrs. Agnes (Marceau) Comes At Night was the spouse of George Comes-at-Night. One of her brother was George "Duffy" Comes At Night. Source: www.legacy.com/obituaries/greatfallstribune/obituary.aspx?n=evelyn-m-no-runner&pid=118895448 (last consulted in June 2018).
- This was Robert Scriver (1920-1998), sculptor and a lot more. From 1950 to 1969 he was also Police Magistrate for the Town of Browning and Justice of the Peace (Strachan 2008: 157, 347).
- The Starr School area is located at the south portion of the Blackfeet Reservation, five miles west of Browning. In 2010 it had a population of 252, with 67 housing units. Source: www.anishinabe-history.com/communities/starr-school.shtml (last consulted in July 2018).
- Levi (Lewis) Aims Back was a half-brother of Aims Back, 38 years (DeMarce 1980: 18).

Page 19
- Arrowtop is now a community, 1.7 miles north of North Browning: "It is named after a street which runs through the area. Its population is included with the population of

Browning's zip code area. However, it is a distinct community. Several hundred people live there." Source: familysearch.org/wiki/en/Blackfeet_Indian_Reservation_(Montana) (last checked in July 2018).
- The Heart Butte people are listen at: www.accessgenealogy.com/native/blackfeet-indian-reservation.htm

Page 20
- John Aims Back One was a son of Aims Back and Isabelle who later married Eddie Big Beaver. Her second son was also named John, so became John Aims Back II (Hungry Wolf IV 2006: 920).

Page 25
- Mr. Chas [Charles?] Iron Breast could have been the husband of Nellie Different Woman, 40 years (DeMarce 1980: 135).
- Perry Spotted Eagle is mentioned in Hungry Wolf (2006: 1290).

Page 26
- Doig (1978: 203) repeats Tatsey's item about Jesse Blackman and comments: "The Blackfeet seemed to be a rambunctious people; I wondered what they thought of our white faces and gray sheep against the backcloth of their prairie past." Blackman was married to Mary Yellow Owl (DeMarce (1980: 40).

Page 29
- Bill Big Spring, a WWII veteran, was one of the children of Billy (†1930) and Bessie Big Spring († 1936) (Hungry Wolf 2006: 961).
- Philip Sure Chief was 2 years and the son of Sure Chief, 40 years and Bird Wing (DeMarce 1980: 248).

Page 31
- George Crawford, 6 years was a son of Minnie Crawford (Old Kyo), 52 years, full Blood and Daniel Crawford, white (DeMarce 1980: 77).
  It sounds as if Tatsey is here making some fun with his colleague George Comes-at-Night.
- Whether Emmet Brewer is the one named in this add for Blackfoot Beer? See: blackfoot-riverbrewing.com/2016/05/e-trail-pale-ale/ (last consulted in June 2018).
- Harvey Monroe, son of Angus Monroe and Lillie Wren was born in 1915. Source: www.blackfeetgenealogy.com/pafg172.htm (last consulted in June 2018).
- Francis Bull Shoe was married to Lillian Henault (born in 1907), father of John Tatsey and grandfather of Carol Murray-Tatsey.

Page 32
- Bill McMullen was a police officer, mentioned in Strachan Scriver (2008: 150).
- This picture of John and Belle Tatsey was taken in October 1957. Source: Archives & Special Collections, Mansfield Library, University of Montana (98-1093).
- George Edwards was likely the grandfather of George Kipp or Eagle Flag (Hungry Wolf 2006: 683).
- George Kipp, one year old, was a son of Joseph Kipp (1/4 Mandan) and Double Strike, full Piegan (DeMarce 1980: 143).

- Henry Evans, born in 1911, was a son of Joseph Evans, 33 years, ½ Piegan and Mary Evans, full Piegan, 26 years. He married Anne Irene Fast Buffalo. Source: www.mtgenweb.com/pondera/rhondasfamilyfiles/evansfamily.htm (link dead in June 2018).
- Eugene Head Carrier, carpenter, died at the age of 65, in 2007, in Heart Butte. Source: www.legacy.com/obituaries/greatfallstribune/obituary.aspx?n=eugene-head-carrier&pid=86362754 (last consulted in June 2018).

Page 40
- Wolf Point is actually a village at the Missouri River in the Roosevelt county, north-east Montana

Page 46
- Hill 57 is located adjacent to Great Falls, Montana but not within the city limits of Great Falls. Though Hill 57 is not within the 4th Blackfeet Reservation, it is within the original Blackfeet Reservation, which was created on September 17, 1851 and approved on October 17, 1855. And it continues to be an Indian settlement. The last census of Hill 57 is from 1956. Hill 57 had a population of over 400 in 1956. The current population is unknown. Source: familysearch.org/wiki/en/Blackfeet_Indian_Reservation_(Montana) (last accessed in June 2018). Paul (2015: 33) presents an interesting section about Hill 57.

Page 49
- Robert Still Smoking was 4 years, son of Joseph and Winnie Still Smoking (DeMarce 1980: 245).

Page 50
- Linda Hirst is a daughter of Clarence Joseph Hirst Sr. (1920) and Minnie Rutherford, both of Heart Butte. Source: wc.rootsweb.ancestry.com/cgi-bin/igm.cgi?op=GET&db=tsmith&id=I222042 (last consulted in July 2018).

Page 53
- John Harper was a representative of the "Blackfoot improvement association."
- Vic Connolly was a representative of the "Blackfoot improvement association."
- According to Paul (2015: 56) oral history indicated "something bad" had been buried within tribal lands. The areas that were repeatedly spoken about were Hudson Bay Divide Ridge, Del Bonita Road, Kiowa Camp and the Four Horn or Owl Child Lake area. Additionally, Boulder Ridge was added to the list of possible contamination events and was placed in the "late seventies ... early eighties" (Running Crane, 2011).

Page 54
- "Records have also been found that implicate a non-tribal member, Hugh Black. This written account suggests that Hugh Black contracted with a government contractor to allow dumping on lands that he had 'purchased' within the Blackfeet Nation" (Paul 2009: 6). About the identity of the white man, Paul (2009: 56) notes that "Plat records verify that this same non-Blackfeet, Hugh Black, had gained ownership of much of the Hudson Bay Divide Ridge area."
- In 2010 a place called "Wippert" is located over 1 mile south of South Browning. Most of the housing units are mobile homes. It's population is included with Browning's zip code

area. Several hundred people live in this fast growing community. Source: familysearch.org/wiki/en/Blackfeet_Indian_Reservation_(Montana) (last accessed in June 2018).

Page 56
- George Horn was 42 years and married first to Annie Bob Tail Horse, later with Susie Horn. They had two children, Charles, 4 years and Joseph 2 years (DeMarce 1980:13). Was there was a third child, George?
- This Republican could have been TIm. M. Babcock, Governor from January 25, 1962 to January 6, 1969. But he must been inaugurated in 1962, on 25 January. Not clear who it can have been. See: en.wikipedia.org/wiki/List_of_Governors_of_Montana (last accessed in June 2018).
- Gordon Dubray was born in 1899 in Fort Macleod and died in 1964 in Glacier Country. Source: www.findagrave.com/memorial/147149972/gordon-dubray (last consulted in July 2018).

Page 57
- Lyndon B. Johnson served from 1963 until 1969. He was followed by Richard Nixon. In this column Tatsey writes about Republican Governor, Gordon Dubray who died in 1964. It had been a long time since Mansfield had gotten any news from Heart Butte; perhaps Tatsey rounded up some news items in this column.

Page 68
- The time of Lewis & Clark was around 1804. In 1803 President Thomas Jefferson initiated an exploration of newly purchased land and the territory beyond the "great mountains" in the West. He chose Meriwether Lewis (1774-1809) to lead this expedition. Lewis solicited the help of William Clark (1870-1838) and together they formed a diverse military Corps of Discovery that would undertake a two-year journey to the great ocean. Source: www.archives.gov/education/lessons/lewis-clark (last consulted in June 2018).
- For more about John L. Clarke, see: www.rit.edu/~w-dada/paddhd/publicDA/main/artists/JohnClarke/index.htm (last accessed in June 2018).

Page 76
- On June 9, 1911 Mrs. Uhlenbeck noted about grandmother Singing All The Time: "Ik hoorde de grootmoeder Indian songs zingen voor de baby, die soms erg huilde" (translated in Eggermont-Molenaar 2005: 36: "I heard the grandmother sing Indian songs for the baby who sometimes cried vigorously"). On August 15, 1911 she reported that the grandmother had died the previous day.

Let's finish

Let's finish with comments by people that knew John Tatsey and put their thoughts of him and his publications to paper.

Over one hundred years ago Mrs. Uhlenbeck wrote that John, the 17-year old, oldest Tatsey boy, looked like his mother, was quiet and serious, had a beautiful face, a beautiful figure though quite small. The impression one gets from her diary entrees about John confirms this. More than once we see John entering the Uhlenbecks' tent, quietly telling Uhlenbeck about his daily activities, assisting him with lexical and translating tasks and then leaving as quietly to resume his cattle chases and other daily occupations.

According to John's granddaughter, Carol Murray-Tatsey, her great-grandfather Joseph Tatsey: "was hired to be the main translator, but a lot of the work he was supposed to do, was actually done by his son John, my grandfather. Joe would often be gone to Browning, Helena, or elsewhere on other business (cited in Hungry Wolf 2006 II: 685)."

Prairie Mary who came to Browning in 1961 to teach English at the Blackfeet high school, blogged in 2005 that "Tatsey's columns came out of his vocation as the tribal policeman in Heart Butte, a tiny village near the Rockies where old ways held on in spite of drunkenness and violence. His columns note a mixture of the two, more like Steinbeck's "Tortilla Flats" than Will Rogers, if you ask me."[21]

Prairie Mary, got a number of responses to this blog, for example this one: "John was certainly colorful." Prairie Mary replied, "John was certainly colorful. Whether he was admirable is up for grabs. As for what he wrote, standards have changed over the years."

---

21. On March 17, 2018 Prairie Mary gracefully gave me consent, by telephone, to quote from her blogs.

Carol Murray-Tatsey about her grandfather John Tatsey (cited in Hungry Wolf II 2006: 685).

> My grandpa John was a policeman down at the Heart Butte community for many years. He did a lot of writing at the time, mostly for the local papers, he ended up getting a book of his stories published by the title, "Black Moccasin." He was a very jolly man - constant laughter. He was a gentle man, but I never thought of him as a writer, or anything like that.
>
> My grandparents at a lot of suppers with us. My grandma was a short woman — maybe five feet tall. When they drove up, we kids rush to help them out of their pick-up, so they wouldn't slide to the ground. At holiday dinners, he would sing Indian songs for us. He was known as a good singer. He even owned a machine that would let him cut records. They lived in a log house and he made his own recordings. I don't know where they all ended up. We were just young then, so after they left the house, others took all of the stuff.

By the end of the year 2012, Mrs. Maizie Upham, Blackfeet, turned 87. This was a reason for Glacier Reporter John McGill to interview her about her life and the changes she's seen throughout. Mrs. Upham told him to have lived all her life at Heart Butte, where she started school at the age of seven. As there was no kindergarten at the time, she had gone to first grade right away.

Mrs. Upham continued about the school, about Tatsey's jail and yes, about her admiration for John. The interview continued like this:

> The town had its own agency, plus a policeman and a jail. She relates that while the Heart Butte cop was paid, his wife, who did all the cooking for the prisoners, was not. [...] Maize was especially proud of Heart Butte Policeman John Tatsey, whose stories were read aloud into the Congressional Record by then-Senator Mike Mansfield and many of which were recorded in a book of his collected writings.
>
> "He was so funny in his words and his actions," she said. "When he talked Indian, he talked about what happened." Upham noted some of his favorite characters to write about were Stoles Head Carrier and George Day Rider.

"John was a kind man," she said. "He'd just lock them up overnight and send them off to Browning. "We're going to drop you off at John Walters' hotel [the Browning jail]," he would say, "and you'll get a job there."

"People from all over from out of state would come just to meet John Tatsey because of that book, and after they met him they thought he was the greatest man. He talked about what happened and the funny things people did, but he never abused anybody," Maizie said.

About 102 years after Mrs. Uhlenbeck wrote about John Tatsey, Prairie Mary blogged about him again: "John's surprising grammar and deadpan sense of humor were very popular and he built quite a mythology about the Napi-like (coyote/trickster like) antics of local people drinking, gambling, racing horses, and chasing or being chased by women. His favorite butt of jokes was "Stoles" (Stanislaus) Head Carrier, a large gentle man who loved drink and gambling. I saw him once, seated on a blanket playing cards while babies sat and lay all around him, left by mothers who knew he would stay there and watch them."

x

List of illustrations

Abbreviations:
- Museum van Volkenkunde Leiden MvVL
- Glenbow Archives Calgary GAC

PART I
- C. C. Uhlenbeck and Willy Uhlenbeck-Melchior ça 1900; photo Binger's Haarlem, Rijksbureau voor Kunsthistorische Documentatie, Den Haag IBO1010098
- John Tatsey 1911; photo Willy Uhlenbeck-Melchior, MvVL (413Cb7c)
- Grandmother and Lizzy 1911; photo Willy Uhlenbeck-Melchior, MvVL (413Cb7b)
- Willy Kennedy 1911; photo Willy Uhlenbeck-Melchior, MvVL (413Cb6c)
- Holy Family Mission, schoolhouse and church; Marquette Archives, Milwaukee, around 1911
- Joe and Annie Tatsey 1911; photo Willy Uhlenbeck-Melchior, MvVL (413Cb5b)
- John Tatsey with Uhlenbeck 1911; photo Willy Uhlenbeck-Melchior, MvVL (413Cb7b)
- Peter and Mary Bear Legging 1911; photo Willy Uhlenbeck-Melchior, MvVL (413Cb8c)
- Bear Chief, around 1900-1905; GAC., photo N.A. Forsyth, Butte Montana, NA-1461-43
- Nieuwe Rijn 69 in Leiden in 2015; photo Mary Eggermont-Molenaar

PART II
- John and Belle Tatsey and Mike Mansfield; photo NAID 37489831, Archives & Special Collections, Mansfield Library, University of Montana (98-1093)
- Mike Mansfield and Lyndon Johnson; Mike Mansfield Archives & Special Collections. University of Montana. (98-1438)
- Lame Bear and John Mountain chief; image courtesy of Peel's Prairie Provinces (peel.library.ualberta.ca)

PART III
- Tatsey 1 - Cover; oil painting Belva Curtis
- Tatsey 1a - Cover picture
- Tatsey 2 - p. 7 - John Tatsey and Sioux wife Belle; photo Wayne Curtis
- Tatsey 3 - p. 10 - John Tatsey and Stoles Head Carrier; photo Wayne Curtis
- Tatsey 4 - p. 12 - Indian policeman John Tatsey; drawing Albert Racine
- Tatsey 5 - P, 15 - John Tatsey and his home; photo Wayne Curtis
- Tatsey 6 - p. 14 - Mrs. Maxime Racine, Mose Henault; drawing Albert Racine
- Tatsey 7 - p. 18 - Levi Aims Back, Soles Head Carrier; drawing Albert Racine
- Tatsey 8 - p. 21 - Tom Lame Bear, A young stockman; drawing Albert Racine
- Tatsey 9 - p. 24 - Loving husbands, Louie Red Head; drawing Albert Racine
- Tatsey 10 - p. 27 - Two moose, Stoles Head Carrier; drawing Albert Racine
- Tatsey 11 - p. 30 - Tribal office on fire, Joe New Robe; drawing Albert Racine
- Tatsey 12 - p. 33 - Indian stick game; photo Wayne Curtis
- Tatsey 13 - p. 34 - Joe New Robe and his team, Philip Dog Gun; drawing Albert Racine
- Tatsey 14 - p. 36 - Belva Curtis and Belle Tatsey; photo Wayne Curtis

- Tatsey 15 – p. 38 – Stoles Head Carrier missing, Joe Running Crane; drawing Albert Racine
- Tatsey 16 – p. 41 – Paul Running Crane, Dog catcher; drawing Albert Racine
- Tatsey 17 – p. 45 – Skeleton last tribal medicine lodge; photo Wayne Curtis
- Tatsey 18 – p. 44 – Heart Butte reporter, Rumpus along Big Badger; drawing Albert Racine
- Tatsey 19 – p. 48 – Peter Stabs by Mistake; photo Wayne Curtis
- Tatsey 20 – p. 49 – Stoles Head Carrier, Geo. Bremner, Robert Still Smoking; drawing Albert Racine
- Tatsey 21 – p. 52 – Glacier Reporter forgetful; Geo. Aims Back drawing Albert Racine
- Tatsey 22 – p. 52 – Buster Yellow Kidney, John Tatsey; drawing Albert Racine
- Tatsey 23 – p. 58 – Mountain Chief; photo Devore
- Tatsey 24 – p. 62 – Blackfeet Indian nation road sign, tanning of hides; photo Wayne Curtis
- Tatsey 25 – p. 65 – Badger Creek valley
- Tatsey 26 – p. 70 – Indians in tribal regalia; photo Paul T. Devore
- Tatsey 27 – Back Cover

Bibliography

Black, Hugh M. 1960. Dissertation. *The history of the Holy Family Mission, Montana, from 1890- 1935.* St. Paul: Minnesota. (pp. 256).

Blackfeet Tribal Business Council and Roxanne De Marce. 1998. *Blackfeet Genealogy, Treasures and Gifts.* Browning: The Blackfeet Tribal Business Council P.O. Box 850. (pp. 429).

Doig, Ivan. 1978. *This House of Sky: Landscapes of a Western Mind.* New York: Harcourt, Inc. (pp. 336).

Fuller, Thomas P. 1898. "Census of the Piegan Indians of Blackfeet Agency, Montana taken by Thomas P. Fuller United States Indian Agent 1898," in *Census of the Blackfeet Montana, 1897-1898* by Jef Bowen. Baltimore: Clearfield Company, Inc. National Archives Microfim Roll M595-4, Indian Census Rolls 1885-1940: Blackfeet Agency, 1897-1906. See: books.google.ca

Britten, Thomas A. 2014 *The National Council on Indian Opportunity.* Albuquerque: University of New Mexico Press. (pp.337). See: muse.jhu.edu/book/33397

De Josselin de Jong, J.P.B. 1912 a. "De dansen der Peigan," in *Onze Eeuw (Our Century)* 12,8:201-230 and 12.9:369-396. Reproduced in *Montana 1911: A Professor and his Wife among the Blackfeet* (pp. 375-398). Ed. Mary Eggermont-Molenaar. Calgary: University of Calgary Press / Lincoln: University of Nebraska Press.

—— 1912 c "Social organization of the southern Peigans," in *IAfE* 20,4:191-197.

—— 1913 a Dissertation. *De waarderingsonderscheiding van "levend" en "levenloos" in Indogermaansch vergeleken met hetzelfde verschijnsel in enkele Algonkin-talen. Ethno-psychologische studie.* (The Evaluative Distinction between "Animate" and "Inanimate" in Indo-Germanic, compared with the similar phenomenon in some Alsonquian language). Leiden: Gebroeders van der Hoek. (224 p.).

—— 1913 b. "Prof. C. C. Uhlenbeck's latest contribution to Blackfoot Ethnology," in *Internationales Archiv für Ethnographie* 21, 2:

105-1915. Review of C. C. Uhlenbeck: *A New Series of Blackfoot Texts*. Amsterdam: KAW 1912.

—— 1914. *Blackfoot Texts from the Southern Peigans Blackfoot Reservation Teton County Montana*. With the Help of Black-Horse-Rider. Verhandelingen der KAW. Afdeeling Letterkunde. NR XIV, nr. 4. Amsterdam: Johan Müller. (pp. 153).

DeMarce, Roxanne. 1980. *Blackfoot Heritage. Allotment 1907-1908.* Browning: Blackfoot Heritage Program. (pp. 287).

Eggermont-Molenaar, Mary. Ed. Transl. 2005. *Montana 1911: A Professor and His Wife among the Blackfeet.* With contributions of Alice Kehoe, Inge Genee and Klaas van Berkel. Calgary: University of Calgary Press. Lincoln: University of Nebraska Press. (pp. 417).

—— 2015. "The correspondence between Wilhelmina Maria Uhlenbeck and Hugo Schuchardt," in Bernhard Hurch (Hg.) (2007-). *Hugo Schuchardt Archiv.* See: schuchardt.unigraz.at/korrespondenz/briefe/korrespondenzpartner/alle/1206/

—— 2015. *Bij de Blackfeet in Montana in 1911. Dagboek van Willy Uhlenbeck-Melchior.* Leiden: Ginkgo. (pp. 252).

Eltringham, Jennifer. 2016. "Cutting Capers on the Sands of North Africa: A Soldier's Art before, during and after World War II." Blog posted on November 10. Also: text-message.blogs.archives.gov/2016/11/10/cutting-capers-on-the-sands-of-north-africa-a-soldiers-art-before-during-and-after-world-war-ii/

Hansen, Pat. 2002. "Peace officers honored," in *Montana Standard* of May 15. mtstandard.com/news/local/peace-officers-honored/article_ecd99daa-b497-5b50-84b9-ecc227a509a8.html

Hungry Wolf, Adolf. 2006. *The Blackfoot Papers.* Vols. I-IV. Skookumchuck: Good Medicine Books.

Jacobs, Frank. 1964. "This Cattleman, [Roy Doore]," in *Canadian Cattlemen* 27 (10): 5+ October.

Lambert, Bruce. 1993. February 28. "Fletcher Knebel, Writer, Dies; Co-Author of 'Seven Days in May,'" in *The New York Times*.

Lawrence, Tom. 2003. *Pictures, a Park, and a Pulitzer: Mel Ruder and the Hungry Horse News.* Helena: Farcountry Press. (pp. 200).

Mansfield, Mike. 1957/1958. "On John Tatsey" at: www.mtmemory.org/cdm/ref/collection/p16013coll41/id/278

McGill, John. 2012, July 25. "Maizie Upham relates personal history of Blackfeet County," in *Glacier Reporter*.

Mike Mansfield Papers: Series 21, Box 39, Folder 6, Mansfield Library, University of Montana. See: cdm103401.cdmhost.com/cdm/ref/collection/p16013coll41/id/278 (last consulted in June 2018).

Prairie Mary (Mary Strachan-Scriver). 2005. "Browning, Montana" in: prairiemary.blogspot.ca/2005/04/browning-montana.html

—— 2005. "JOHN TATSEY," in: prairiemary.blogspot.ca/2005/06/john-tatsey.html

—— 2007. "HOLY FAMILY MISSION by Hugh Black (notes)," at: prairiemary.blogspot.ca/2007/04/holy-family-mission-by-hugh-black-notes.html

—— 2009. "Napi and the Aggregator," at: prairiemary.blogspot.ca/2009/09/napi-and-aggregator.html

—— 2015. "Blackfeet Myths and Legends" at: prairiemary.blogspot.com/2015/09/blackfeet-myths-and-legends.html

Rides at the Door, Darnell. 1979. *Napi Stories*. Browning: Blackfeet Heritage Program. (pp. 38).

Strachan-Scriver, Mary. 2006. *Twelve Blackfoot Stories*. Valier: Self-published.

—— 2007. *Bronze. Inside and Out: A Biographical Memoir of Bob Scriver*. Calgary: University of Calgary Press. (pp. 392).

Tatsey, John. 1971. "Life on the Blackfeet Indian Reservation as recorded by John Tatsey," in *The Black Moccasin*. Compiled and edited by Paul T. DeVore. Spokane: Curtis Art Gallery, Davenport Hotel (pp. 79).

Thompson, Bob & Hugh Johnson. 1976. *The California Wine Book*. New York. William Morrow and Company, Inc. (pp. 320).

Uhlenbeck, C. C. 1885. *Gedachten en droomen* (Dreams and thoughts). Haarlem: I. de Haan (pp. 152)

—— 1906 "Zur Eskomogrammatick [!]" in *Zeitschrift der Deutschen Morgenlandischen Gesellschaft* 60: 112-114.

—— 1908. "Die einheimischen Sprachen Nord-Amerikas bis zum Rio Grande," in *Anthropos* 3: 773-799.

—— 1909. "Grammatical distinctions in Algonquian demonstrated especially in the Ojibway dialect," in *Anthropos* 5: 607

—— 1910. "Ontwerp van eene vergelijkende vormleer van eenige Algonkin-talen," in *Verhandelingen der KAW*, Afdeeling Letterkunde, Nieuwe Reeks, Deel XI. No 3. Amsterdam: Noord-Hollandse Uitgevers-maatschappij. (pp. 67).

—— Translated from Dutch to English, introduced and annotated by Joshua Snider (2013) as *Outline for a Comparative Grammar of Some Algonquian Languages [Ojibway, Cree, Micmac, Natick and Blackfoot]*. Petoskey MI: Mundart Press.

—— 1911. *Original Blackfoot Texts. From the Southern Peigans Blackfoot Reservation, Teton Country, Montana*. With the help of Joseph Tatsey, in *Verhandelingen der KAW*, Afdeeling Letterkunde, Nieuwe Reeks, Deel XII. No 1. (pp. 106).

—— 1913. "Flexion of Substantives in Blackfoot: A Preliminary Sketch," in *Verhandelingen der KAW*. Afdeeling Letterkunde. Nieuwe Reeks, Deel XIV, no 1. Amsterdam: Noord- Hollandse Uitgeversmaatschappij.

—— 1916. "Some Blackfoot Songs," in *Internationales Archiv für Ethnographie* 23: 241-42.

—— 1920. "A Survey of the Non-Pronominal and Non-Formative Affixes of the Blackfoot Verb: A Contribution to the Knowledge of Algonquian Word-Formation," in *Verhandelingen der KAW*, Afdeeling Letterkunde. Nieuwe Reeks, Deel XX. No. 2. (pp. 132).

—— 1925a. "Nieuwe woorden in het Blackfoot," in *Mededeelingen der KAW*, Deel 59, Serie A: 199-215.

—— 1925b. "Some word-comparisons between Blackfoot and other Algonquian languages," in *International Journal of American Languages* (IJAL) 3(1): 103-8.

—— 1925c. "Blackfoot *imitá(ua)*, dog," in *International Journal of American Languages* 3: 236.

—— 1927. "De afwezigheid der datief-conceptie in het Blackfoot," in *Symbolis grammaticis in honorem Ioannis Radowski*. (pp. 71-82).

—— 1938. *A Concise Blackfoot Grammar, based on material from the Southern Peigans,* in *Verhandelingen der KAW,* Afdeeling Letterkunde, Nieuwe Reeks. 41. Amsterdam: N.V. Noord-Hollandsche Uitgevers-Maatschappij. (pp. 240).

www.ingramcontent.com/pod-product-compliance
Lightning Source LLC
Chambersburg PA
CBHW020934090426
42736CB00010B/1141